THE ULTIMATE NEW YORK BODY PLAN

DAVID KIRSCH

Exercise photographs by Shonna Valeska

McGraw-Hill

New York Chicago San Francisco
Lisbon London Madrid Mexico City Milan
New Delhi San Juan Seoul Singapore
Sydney Toronto

*The **McGraw·Hill** Companies*

9 0   DOC/DOC   0 9 8 7 6 5

ISBN: 0-07-144649-4

This book is for educational purposes. It is not intended as a substitute for individual fitness, health, and medical advice. Please consult a qualified health care professional for individual health and medical advice. Neither McGraw-Hill nor the author shall have any responsibility for any adverse effects that arise directly or indirectly as a result of the information provided in this book.

McGraw-Hill books are available at special quantity discounts to use as premiums and sales promotions, or for use in corporate training programs. For more information, please write to the Director of Special Sales, Professional Publishing, McGraw-Hill, Two Penn Plaza, New York, NY 10121-2298. Or contact your local bookstore.

Interior exercise photographs copyright © by Shonna Valeska.

 This book is printed on recycled, acid-free paper containing a minimum of 50% recycled de-inked fiber.

To Bonnie—
Believe in yourself as I believe in you.

CONTENTS

Kenna lost 10 pounds and shrunk her waist by 2 inches, her hips by $1\frac{1}{2}$ inches, and her arms by 1 inch.

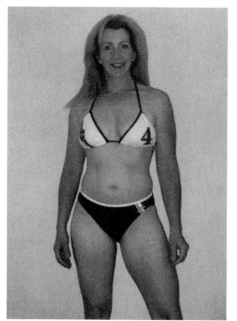

Michel lost 15 pounds and shrunk her clothing size from a 16 to an 8.

PREFACE

It has been a few years since I wrote my first book, *Sound Mind, Sound Body*. I faced writing another book with great trepidation. I was no longer a neophyte author. The more one knows about the process of writing a book, the more daunting is the task of writing another. I had presented a lot of information in the first book and wasn't sure I had more to say. As you will soon see, I did have lots to say, and the program I developed for *The Ultimate New York Body Plan* is short in duration but long in effect.

I have approached this task very much like many others in my life—in a methodical, organized manner. When considering whether to take on the project, I pondered the same questions that concerned me the first time around: "What are my objectives in writing this book? What are the thoughts and feelings that I want to resonate long after the last page is read?"

I ruminated over these questions after appearing on the highly popular television series "Extreme Makeover." In this show, men and women are teamed up with a personal trainer and plastic surgeon; these professionals are charged with the task of taking them from flabby to fit, fat to slender, sun-damaged to radiant, all within a very short period of time. The show taught me that many men and women—perhaps you are one of them—are looking for a quick fix and a fast way to transform their bodies.

For many years, I didn't believe in quick fixes. I told my clients that they had to stick with me for at least six weeks before they would see major results. The "Extreme Makeover" challenge of training and transforming four women in a short period of time opened up a new universe to me. I realized that many people, given the right exercise and nutrition plan, can achieve stunning results in as little as two weeks. Even more important, if they stick with the right maintenance plan, something the "Extreme Makeover" show does not develop, they can maintain these results for life.

For the "Extreme Makeover" show, I worked with four women ranging in age from 32 to 56 and in body weight from a low of 100 pounds to a high of 175. Their body fat percentages ranged from 25 percent to 38 percent, and their physical condition varied as well. One woman had not worked out or done anything physical in many years. Another was a semipro tennis player. Add into the mix a woman who had been training as a power lifter and another who needed to gain weight and muscle on her slight 100-pound frame. Each came from a different socioeconomic background; two were single mothers, and one, the mother of two young children.

Yet, as different as they were, they shared a common bond. They all had body issues and self-esteem issues. The women had different physical issues and body types, but all longed to look and feel better and were willing to endure extreme measures to obtain their desired looks. As a result, they had already endured extensive plastic surgery when I met them.

I met Michel first. She's from the Northeast and had worked out in the past. I took one look at her large, muscular frame and knew she had been power lifting. To give Michel the body she desired, I was going to have to change her attitude toward working out. As is often the case, unlearning bad habits or incorrect gym practices is often more challenging than teaching someone something new, like the difference between a lunge and a squat. (One view of me on the tennis court a couple of years ago would confirm this fact.) In Michel's favor was the fact that she had the desire and, for the most part, the strength and willpower to persevere. In addition to her workout practices, her diet left much to be desired. She liked her carbohydrates, fast food, soda, and, as I would soon find out, New York City street vendor hot dogs. This would never do. My philosophy is predicated on the integration of mind and body with good nutrition and disciplined and consistent exercise. Her poor nutrition coupled with her inappropriate training style resulted in blocky, masculine muscles and way too much body fat. I needed to help her trim and sculpt her muscles while simultaneously reducing the fat to make her look and feel more feminine with a longer, sexier, more streamlined body. Taking people outside of themselves and their preconceived notions of what they are meant to look like is challenging, but the biggest doubter can be turned into a believer with the right mind-set, hard work, and perseverance.

Because of the recovery period that followed surgery, I had only two and one-half weeks to work my magic. We did have one factor in our favor. Michel had been on my nutrition plan just prior to the surgery and remained on the plan throughout the program. The combination of the fairly strict nutrition plan along with my cardio sculpting workout (Chapter 3) produced astonishing results. In just over two weeks of strenuous workouts, Michel became one of my greatest triumphs. She lost more than 30 pounds and 10 percent of her body fat. She dropped from a dress size 16 to a size 8.

For doubters who think this is just another fad program where such incredible results will quickly disappear, I'd like to share with you a telephone call I received one month after I had finished working with Michel. I had called to check in and was ecstatic when she told me she had remained true to our hard work together and had dropped another dress size (down to a size 6)! Another dress size in one month, and she was training on her own and following the nutrition guidelines that I had set for her. A year after the program, Michel has continued to maintain her results. She is the walking embodiment of what my Ultimate Makeover program is all about. Her goals when she met me were to look and feel more feminine, have more energy, and discover and understand how she might maintain and incorporate these principles into her everyday life. I can proudly say that Michel's life is transformed.

My next "Extreme Makeover" client was Samantha, a single mother in her fifties who had not done much for herself in many years, if ever. She had focused on rearing and supporting her children as a young, single mother, which had left her little or no time to focus on her physical or mental well-being. When I met her, she was scared, tentative, and somewhat skeptical toward the whole transformation process. She was looking forward to the results that the plastic surgery would bring and took to my food philosophy easily. The exercise component was another story. Unlike Michel, Samantha did not embrace the exercise component, and she doubted that exercise could transform her fifty-something-year-old body.

By the time we started working out together, Samantha had been on my nutrition program for almost three weeks. I used kid gloves when explaining my exercise program, fearing that the talk of sumo lunges and plié squats would have her bolting for the door. I asked her to define what, if anything, she hoped to achieve through working with me. These question-and-answer sessions made me realize that I could break through Samantha's wall of fear.

Of all the women I've worked with, Samantha was the most deeply sensitive. Life had dealt her a pretty rough hand, and she brought a lot of vulnerability and emotion into our training sessions. It wasn't uncommon for Samantha to break down and cry in the middle of a session. At times, her tears were of fear and apprehension, but more often, as we progressed, they were of appreciation and exultation. Samantha reminded me of many of my clients. After years of inactivity—caring for the kids, working, and just not finding the time to devote to wellness—they often appear somewhat reluctant at first, but ultimately are transformed. For the first time in her life, Samantha was connecting her mind and her body. She was feeling alive and young again, as if she had been trapped for years in her old body. In 15 days of training with me, Samantha lost almost 10 pounds and went from 38 percent body fat to 28 percent. She lost an amazing 21 pounds of fat. That's not bad for a 56-year-old woman who had not exercised in more than 30 years! The most exciting thing for me was that I was able to transform a nonexercise person into someone who not only recognized the benefits of movement, good nutrition, and exercise, but who also embraced them. The idea that Samantha will—like the seventies Breck commercial—tell two friends and so on and so on, spreading the "word," makes me feel proud for having participated in the program.

Kenna, an avid tennis player, had a classic apple shape. Although she was athletic, both her fitness efforts and nutrition needed tweaking. Kenna eagerly and conscientiously embraced my principles and transformed her body and her life. She has gone back to the tennis court with renewed vigor and has returned to the dating scene with a newfound confidence.

The fourth woman I worked with, Denise, was the youngest of the four and had a unique problem. Unlike the others, she needed to add weight and curves (in the form of muscle) to her body. She weighed barely 100 pounds and had often been confused for a boy. Being myself of lean body, I felt her pain and frustration. She had had extensive plastic surgery, including breast augmentation, so we were really forced to focus on her lower half. By the end of the program, she had gained an impressive six pounds while reducing her body fat by almost 8 pounds, resulting in a more curvaceous figure.

Michel, Samantha, Denise, and Kenna all benefited physically, mentally, and spiritually on my Ultimate Makeover program—and so can you. After completing the program, all four women realized that the real bonus was in rediscovering their physical and spiritual balance. The lessons they learned while with me at the Madison Square Club will last them a lifetime. They gained more than just superficial beauty (which may fade in time); this program has enabled and empowered them to live and be more productive, prosperous, and healthy on every level imaginable. Additionally, the lessons I learned have transformed my life.

After working with the "Extreme Makeover" women, I soon began training my regular clientele differently, offering this new two-week plan to anyone who wanted to get buff in a short period of time. In every instance, my clients dropped stunning amounts of body fat, sculpted beautiful muscle, and, within just two weeks, got in the best shape of their lives. You will find some of their stunning success stories in Chapter 5.

Whatever your goal, say a last-minute tune-up for a wedding, getting ready for bikini weather, or shaping up post pregnancy, my Ultimate New York Body Plan will take you where you need to go. This program provides the ultimate in mind and body transformation.

To complete this program, you will need an incredible amount of discipline, drive, and willingness to push your body to places it has never gone before. You will need to accept the notion that good health, better energy, and feeling and looking better all contribute to your willpower and motivation. These principles are essential to the two-week program set forth in *The Ultimate New York Body Plan*. You'll learn everything you need for success within the pages of this book.

Although the two-week program in *The Ultimate New York Body Plan* is extreme, with very stringent nutrition and exercise guidelines, sound philosophy must prevail. The principles of *Sound Mind, Sound Body* have provided the foundation of this program. You'll achieve stunning results in a short period of time, but you will also eat healthful foods and lose weight in a safe way. *The Ultimate New York Body Plan* will feed you with the knowledge you need, motivate you to push harder, and give you the strength, intelligence, and confidence to maintain your results for life.

■ ■ ■

At the conclusion of *Sound Mind, Sound Body*, I remember agonizing over the acknowledgments. My greatest fear was somehow forgetting and unintentionally slighting someone by failing to specifically mention them. I promised myself that if I got a second chance—how many of us actually do—I wasn't going to make the same mistake. The problem is, the more I thought about it, the more daunting the task. The solution: Keep it short and simple.

I have spent the better part of the last two decades devoting myself to helping people transform their lives as they transformed their bodies. *The Ultimate New York Body Plan* is just one of the programs I have developed. In the process, I, too have been transformed. I have had the great honor and privilege of working with clients who have trusted and believed in my abilities, and with their trust and loyalty, have given me the strength, courage and motivation to continue exploring and developing my life's passion—your generosity, kindness, and allegiance have made this all possible and enriched me beyond all measure. It is with undying gratitude that I acknowledge and thank each and every one of my clients (past, present and future)—for without you, none of this would be possible. Of course, in this category are the 14 makeover subjects whom I've included in this book. With your sweat and tenacity, you helped give *The Ultimate New York Body Plan* its identity. Amy, Bonnie, Danielle, Debra, Gali, Heidi, Jonathan, Kenna, Kenny, Marcy, Michel, Pam, Sam, and Todd—I give you my love and undying gratitude. Thank you for believing in me as I always believed in you.

I founded and created the Madison Square Club 15 years ago because I thought New York was ready for a full-service, boutique personal training club. Personal training facilities need personal trainers—I couldn't possibly do it by myself. I am truly blessed to have the best trainers; with their intelligence, devotion, loyalty, and great skills, they have helped maintain the club's status as one of the finest in the country. I would like to offer my most heartfelt thanks and appreciation to Adam, Alex, Alfonso, David, Dawn, Mike, Robert, Ronnie, Sean, and Steve. And also to Abul, Aktar, Anna, Aurelio, Avital, Elie, Jessica, Meital, and Sheffie for streamlining and facilitating the running of my club and for keeping my life reasonably organized.

I would like to thank everyone at McGraw-Hill for working so hard on this project and for truly understanding what The Ultimate New York Body Plan is all about. I am proud to be one of your authors and hope to make you proud of me. I would like to thank Nancy Hancock for bringing me to McGraw-Hill and for believing in me once again. I would be remiss if I didn't acknowledge the terrific job Michele Pezzuti has done since taking over as my editor. I will never forget our first photo shoot together. And speaking of photo shoots, my love and appreciation to my friend Shonna for, once again, going above and beyond. Your photographs are, as always, perfect.

Thanks also to my friend and second brain Alisa Bauman for her tireless work and brilliant assistance in writing this book. I couldn't have completed this book without you. You helped make sense of it all. Thanks to my friend and tastebud genius, Jennifer, who once again came through (even with laryngitis) and converted teaspoons to tablespoons and tested and tasted every one of the recipes in the program.

To Marcy and all the girls at Engelman and Co. and Desiree and all the girls at Full Picture—thank you for your friendship, support, guidance, and love. I am truly blessed to have you in my life.

To Faith, Heidi, Linda, and Liv—your kind and generous thoughts and words of support mean so very much to me—all my love and gratitude.

To Penelope and Leslie for making my crib a home. You gave me what no one else could—my peaceful inner sanctum.

Last, but certainly not least, I must thank and acknowledge my parents and family for their support, encouragement, and love. My ability to love and nurture is a testament to their support of me through the years.

David Kirsch
Web site: www.davidkirsch.com

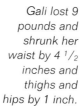

Gali lost 9 pounds and shrunk her waist by 4 $1/2$ inches and thighs and hips by 1 inch.

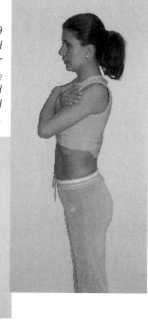

Heidi started working out four weeks after giving birth. In two weeks, she was back in shape.

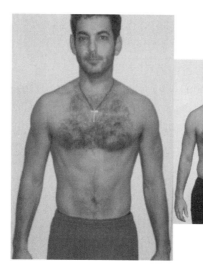

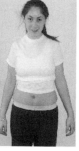

Danielle lost 7 pounds and 5 inches from her waist.

Jonathan lost 8 pounds, shrunk his waist by 2 $3/4$ inches, and increased his arm circumference by 1 inch and his chest by $1/2$ inch.

1
THE ELEMENTS OF
YOUR ULTIMATE SUCCESS

When ABC approached me about participating as the fitness and wellness expert for its popular television show "Extreme Makeover," I felt honored, but also conflicted. The basic philosophy of the show not only included diet and exercise (which I would be in charge of), but also extensive plastic surgery, including nose jobs, brow lifts, liposuction, and face-lifts. I am not opposed to plastic surgery (not that I have or will ever elect to have any), but I didn't want to endorse the notion that someone would need to undergo such extreme and often painful means to look his or her best. That's just not in line with my philosophy as a trainer and wellness coach.

That said, I agreed to participate, and the process helped me to develop the program that eventually grew into this book. My decision was based on my desire to not only transform these women's bodies, but also help them transform their lives. I felt that I could show these women and millions of viewers that one could have a makeover, and a pretty comprehensive one at that, by adhering to the sound eating and exercise principles of my program. Not only was I going to transform their bodies, but I was going to empower them by teaching them how to maintain their results throughout their lives.

My task on the "Extreme Makeover" show was daunting. I was asked to help women completely make over their bodies in just 14 to 21 days. Generally, I suggest a much longer program for body transformation, one that lasts about six weeks. Yet, because the "Extreme Makeover" show wanted extreme results in an extremely short period of time, I modified the traditional nutrition and fitness program that I generally prescribe to my clients. Basically, the nutrition and fitness plan became much more intense. Although all the women had cosmetic surgery, they all agree that it was the workout and the nutrition regimens that still resonate in their everyday lives. They all still follow my training program, albeit maybe not as rigorously, and adhere at least to a certain degree to my nutrition plan.

The results got me thinking. What if I could convince others to embrace the notion that ultimate makeovers were attainable and could be realized with sweat and determination—but no plastic surgery? The Ultimate New York Body Plan was born.

EXTREME VERSUS ULTIMATE RESULTS

My objective here is not to bash the "Extreme Makeover" show. I think the human element in the show is compelling and makes for good television. I haven't watched the program much, but did turn it on one night as I was editing this chapter. There were three makeovers, and the results were pretty extreme. I was pleased to see that the show's producers were finally paying more attention to the physical training aspect, but I was dismayed that they failed to recognize that nutrition is a huge part of the equation. There was another glaring omission as well—the maintenance program. It is great to feature transformations, but if you don't give people the tools necessary to maintain the results, then you're really doing them a disservice.

How do people get to the point where they need extreme makeovers? Why are so many people overweight in America? Why are child obesity rates increasing at such an alarming rate? If you don't get to the root of the unhappiness (and I'm not talking about big noses or saggy bottoms), you are not going to maintain whatever superficial results you may achieve no matter how dramatic they are.

Nutrition counts for up to 70 percent in our overall wellness quotient. I don't care how many push-ups you do. If you are still going to reach for the burger and fries, then all the liposuction in the world will not keep you skinny. For this program, your nutrition plan is just as important—if not more important—than your exercise plan. The biggest distinction between my Ultimate Body Plan and the "Extreme Makeover" program is that I not only train you, but I also feed you and teach you how to incorporate nutrition principles into your everyday life. Remember, makeovers should be about empowerment! With empowerment, you will have the courage, willpower, and fortitude to stay the course.

THE ULTIMATE MAKEOVER

After working on the "Extreme Makeover" show, I began introducing this faster, more extreme program to clients. I had many clients who were very fit and who ate well, but who wanted to take their bodies to the next level. They wanted to look great for bikini season or sculpt their best body for a wedding or upcoming reunion. Often, when they told me of these goals, they would sheepishly look at me and say, "But it's just two weeks away."

Before I worked on the "Extreme Makeover" show and before I began applying what I learned for the show to my everyday clients, I would have told you that two weeks is not enough time to get into shape. I would have talked you out of your desire for fast results and into embarking on a longer, six-week program designed to last a lifetime. Even for the "Extreme Makeover" show, I was at first skeptical of how much could be accomplished in so short a period of time. I'll never forget the look on my clients' faces when I did the final body fat measurements. We all burst into tears! The percentages (although impressive) were only part of the reason. There is something powerful and empowering in helping to transform someone's life. I feel blessed for the opportunity to have worked with these amazing women. They helped transform a skeptic (myself) into a true believer. Even after all these years of personal training, I, too, learned a valuable lesson. Anyone can make over his or her body and life. No one is too big or small, old or young. The makeover, when looked at as a life-transforming experience, delivers the fuel you'll need to drive you through life's toughest travails and challenges.

I believe there are times when it's good to step up your fitness routine and eating plan in order to take your results to the next level. As long as you accept that change—any change—will include physical, mental, and spiritual transformation, then you can do it.

You might be asking yourself how or why I chose two weeks as the length of time for The Ultimate New York Body Plan. I didn't arbitrarily choose this period, nor do I feel that it is necessarily the ideal amount of time to embark on a life-transforming program. First and foremost, it works. Not only have I transformed the "Extreme Makeover" women in this period of time, but you will read about many other men and women whom I transformed with this plan in later chapters of this book. Second, I chose two weeks because it is a long enough period of time to be effective but not so long that it is unduly burdensome or boring. After 16 years of training countless types of individuals—men and women, old and young, celebrities and noncelebrities alike—I've realized that many of us (myself included) often have limited attention spans. In *Sound Mind, Sound Body*, I set forth a six-week life-transforming program. It worked in transforming many people's lives. I now realize, however, that not all people have that much time or willpower to achieve their goals.

Are you ready to sculpt, lift, burn fat, and eat your way to an ultimate makeover in just 14 days? This is a pretty challenging and rigorous program. It is not for the faint of heart—and I mean that literally and figuratively. If you have never exercised before in your life, my core program isn't for you. It requires a strong exercise commitment—an hour to an hour and a half of exercise on most days. It requires you to head into the program with some form of a fitness routine. Yet, if you're currently a couch potato who has never exercised a day in your life, this doesn't mean you can't soon go on the core program. In fact, I've provided a modified program in this chapter that is designed to help you get in great shape. You'll still sculpt sexy muscle and get stronger and leaner. You just won't work at the same level of intensity as you will on the core program. So whether you have been exercising or not, you have everything you need right here to start striving for ultimate results. You may, however, need to take a smaller step forward and do a little work, physically and mentally, before embarking on the core program.

In this chapter, you will find a series of questions and fitness tests that you need to answer and satisfactorily complete before you can proceed with the 14-day program. Although the program is extreme, it is definitely not unsafe for most people. As with any challenging exercise program, it is prudent to consult with your physician before commencing the program. If you are in doubt as to your physical abilities, lean on the side of being more rather than less conservative in deciding when to start the intensive program. Remember, there is no shame in starting with the fitness test and following with the preprogram before going "all out." The program will methodically train your mind and your body and take them to levels that you previously thought impossible.

THE ULTIMATE NEW YORK BODY PLAN

You're about to embark on the three-pronged attack on flab that includes ultimate fitness, ultimate nutrition, and ultimate motivation, followed by ultimate maintenance.

ULTIMATE FITNESS The Ultimate New York Body Plan combines a mixture of cardio sculpting and lightweight and high-repetition resistance training. You will use lightweight dumbbells, a stability ball, a medicine ball, and your own body weight to perform the exercises.

ULTIMATE NUTRITION The nutrition component of The Ultimate New York Body Plan is definitely a little more extreme than my six-week program outlined in *Sound Mind, Sound Body.* Because this program lasts just 14 days, you must minimize calorie consumption and maximize fat and calorie burning. To accomplish this task, you must strictly adhere to my A, B, C, D, E, and F of nutrition, which basically means no alcohol, bread, starchy carbohydrates, dairy products, extra sweets, fruit, and most fats. Yes, as you can see, it's an extreme plan. You will have to give up many of your favorite foods for 14 days. In addition to following the A, B, C, D, E, and F of nutrition, you will drink two protein shakes a day and eat one wholesome meal and two snacks. (Note: for those of you who prefer to eat rather than drink your calories, I have provided food options in place of the shakes.)

Because your body will be under an enormous strain resulting from the extensive exercise and rigorous nutrition plan, I will be recommending that you beef up on your supplements, including antioxidants, minerals, amino acids, and Chinese herbs. If you have never taken any supplements, then you will need to read Chapter 8, Resources, very carefully, as I set forth the choices of supplements currently on the market and indicate some of my favorites. If you are already taking supplements, you may find it necessary to increase the amounts that you are taking.

ULTIMATE MOTIVATION Working out for an hour and a half a day and giving up many of your favorite foods is challenging. That's why, in Chapter 2, I've provided you with the tools you will need to avoid cheating, bingeing, and backsliding. I often find myself giving my clients pep talks over the phone in order to help them stay on track, and this chapter is based on many of those pep talks.

For example, not long ago, I was about to travel on business for a couple of days when I received an emergency call that Michel, one of the "Extreme Makeover" women, was having a rendezvous with mashed potatoes, street vendor hot dogs, and the occasional Häagen-Dazs ice cream cone. Because we had so little time together and were trying to achieve very dramatic results, I knew it was time for one of "those" conversations. We were both working too hard to have her drown in mashed potatoes and vendor hot dogs. Those fast-food demons were calling, and I was ready to answer swiftly and steadily.

I called her into my office late one night after I had finished training and sat her down. We had established a nice rapport, so I just came right out with it: "What's with the mashed potatoes and the dogs?" To her credit, she didn't deny her transgressions and said that she was having difficulty adhering to the stringent guidelines of my food program. I told her, "If it doesn't come in my food bag, you can't put it in your mouth." I told her she had no choice. To keep training with me, she had to follow the rules to the letter of the law. We had no room and, just as important, no time for her little treats. I'm sorry if that sounds a little too "drill sergeant" for you. I promise you, it was a tough message delivered with lots of love. Through this experience Michel gained respect for me for my support and directness and I for her for her candidness and acceptance of the rigid guidelines I was setting forth. She got it, and it never became an issue again.

I'm not proposing that I always adhere to my nutrition tenets and guidelines. But, as I've said repeatedly, this is an extreme two-week program requiring extreme discipline. Make sure you are psyched about making a dramatic change in your body and get ready (as Michel ultimately did) to make some sacrifices. In the end, it will all be worth it. I promise!

ULTIMATE MAINTENANCE I'd be remiss if I sent you out on a two-week Ultimate Body Plan and then failed to provide you with the tools you will need to maintain your results. Although you will not continue to follow as strict a diet or exercise program as you will for 14 days, that doesn't mean you can completely revert to your old ways after the 14 days. During this program you are going to push your body to the edge and beyond. Why backslide as soon as the program is over? Or any time, for that matter? In Chapter 6, you will learn the fundamentals for staying on track after you achieve results. You'll learn how to work some of your favorite foods back into your diet and how to relax a bit on your fitness program—without losing your hard-earned results. I'll provide you with a maintenance menu featuring approximately a dozen food choices that you will be permitted to slowly reintroduce into your nutrition regimen. These will include some choices that are forbidden on the two-week program. You will see how easy it is to eat some of your favorite foods again, but now you will be armed with the knowledge and the confidence to eat more intelligently.

AN HONORING PROCESS

In Chapter 2, I'll ask you to set some goals. Although some of your goals may be purely physical, I hope your overall goal includes a much larger life picture. A friend and client of mine, Jaime King, once said, "Training with David

Kirsch was an honoring process." She meant that she needed to take time out of her busy day to have time for herself, time that was just hers. The training grounded her and fortified and empowered her to face the challenges that were presented to her in other aspects of her life.

I believe that total transformation is possible by adhering to certain tenets. Self-acceptance and self-love are paramount and help contribute to a sense of wellness and, if you will, soundness of mind and soundness of body. Big noses, breasts (small or large), wrinkles, and so on are all a part of life. We can choose to live with them and accept them as a "rite of passage," or we can mourn every perceived flaw and evidence of loss of our youth. The difference is merely one of attitude and gratitude. We can embrace our life and the circumstances surrounding it. Change isn't necessarily a bad thing, although it can be scary. Choose to change the things that truly matter. Learn to focus on the positive, and be grateful for all your blessings. No matter how much you hate your wrinkles, hating them won't make them go away.

I believe that every wrinkle and every gray hair tells a story. The problem is, most of us place too much emphasis on the superficial (wrinkles and such) and not on the more meaningful and long-lasting results of health, fitness, and good nutrition. We lose sight of the things that are most important and get caught on the liposuction treadmill. My hope is that after reading this book, you will see that you don't need to go under the knife to have an ultimate makeover. I believe that a healthy makeover can result in dramatic physical changes. Rather than submit to the knife to achieve these results, you will, as Jaime says, "find the time in your busy day to honor yourself" through some soul-searching and physically challenging and spiritually rewarding exercise and eating. You can and will lose inches, pounds, and percentages of body fat. Your clothes will fit better, and you will have more energy and stamina. Just as important, you will be doing it without the aid of surgery. You will be bettering yourself in a holistic, nurturing way.

The Ultimate New York Body Plan may (and probably will) leave you craving for more. The mores in this instance, however, will be exercise and good nutrition. You will see that the best and longest-lasting results are achieved with that "one-two" punch.

Are You Ready?

In upcoming chapters, you will learn about each element of the program: motivation, fitness, and nutrition. First, however, let's take a moment to assess your readiness to start the program. The Ultimate Body Plan fitness and nutrition plans are extreme and strict. You will need a certain amount of fitness and nutritional know-how going into the core program in order to achieve success. The following tests will help you to assess your physical, mental, and nutritional readiness for the core program of The Ultimate New York Body Plan.

Be realistic and honest. That's the only way to ensure successful completion of this program. If you determine that you are not ready to begin the core program, don't despair. In the following sections you'll find programs to prepare you for your ultimate makeover.

Fitness Test

To assess your readiness for the exercise portion of The Ultimate New York Body Plan, answer the following questions:

1. Can you do a regular freestanding squat 10 to 15 times   **Y**   **N**
without stopping?

(Note: To perform a squat, stand with your feet a shoulder's width apart. With your weight evenly balanced on both feet, bend your knees and sit back over your heels as you push your butt out. Once your thighs are parallel to the floor, rise to standing.)

2. Can you do 10 pushups on your toes without stopping?　　　**Y**　**N**

3. Can you hold yourself in the low position of a push-up　　　**Y**　**N**
for at least 10 seconds?

4. Can you hold yourself in a plank—the "up" position of a　　　**Y**　**N**
push-up—for at least 10 seconds?

5. Can you do 15 deep knee bends without stopping?　　　**Y**　**N**

6. Can you perform 15 lunges on each leg without　　　**Y**　**N**
stopping?

7. Can you perform 20 jumping jacks without feeling pain　　　**Y**　**N**
in your knees or back?

8. Can you sit on a stability ball with your knees bent and feet flat on the floor without losing your balance? Y N

9. From a seated position on a stability ball, can you walk out into a bench press position, with your upper back and shoulders against the ball and feet on the floor and then walk back up to the seated position without losing your balance? Y N

(Note: To walk out into the bench press position, walk your feet forward as you slide your back down the ball until your knees are bent at 90 degree angles and only your upper back, shoulders, and head are in contact with the ball. To rise, walk your feet toward the ball as you slide your torso up.)

10. Can you perform the following cardio routine for five minutes without a break? (See the section "The 'I'm on My Way to the Ultimate Body' Fitness Preprogram" later in this chapter for descriptions of the exercises in this routine.)   Y   N

■ One minute of jumping jacks while holding three-pound dumbbells

■ One minute of crossover punches while holding three-pound dumbbells

■ One minute of uppercut punches while holding three-pound dumbbells

■ One minute of hook punches while holding three-pound dumbbells

■ 15 to 20 squat thrusts

■ 30 seconds of mountain climbers

After you complete the ten-minute sequence, rate how you feel on a scale of 1 to 5:

    (5) I couldn't finish the routine.

    (4) The routine felt intense, but, with time, I will be able to do it.

    (3) The routine felt somewhat intense, but it was also invigorating.

    (2) I got my heart rate up, but could have held a conversation during the routine if need be.

    (1) Was that supposed to be a workout?

Scoring Key: If you answered no to any question 1 through 9 and ranked your exertion a 4 or 5 for question 5, you are not physically ready to start the core program of the Ultimate Body Plan. Turn to the section titled "The 'I'm on My Way to the Ultimate Body' Fitness Preprogram" later in this chapter for a two-week program that will get you in shape but won't tax your body quite as extensively as the Ultimate Body Plan. Go ahead and start your Ultimate Body Nutrition Plan along with the two-week "I'm on My Way to the

Ultimate Body" Fitness Preprogram. In two weeks, you'll experience dramatic results—and you'll be ready to reassess your physical readiness for the core program. If you're still not ready, you can follow the same program, reassessing every two weeks, until you achieve the physical abilities to work in an extreme way. Don't feel discouraged if you are not physically ready today, two weeks from now, or even six weeks from now. You will still be exercising and improving your fitness—and body—with a routine that fits your current fitness level. You'll see results at every level.

NUTRITIONAL READINESS

1. How many meals do you eat a day?
   A Two or fewer.
   B Three.
   C Four or more.

2. How often do you drink diet or regular soda or fruit juice?
   A Not an hour goes by that I don't have a soda can in my hand.
   B I drink soda or fruit juice with every meal.
   C I rarely drink soda or fruit juice.

3. What is your relationship with fast food?
   A I can't drive past a fast-food restaurant without pulling into the drive-through.
   B I have a busy lifestyle and eat fast food three or four times a week out of necessity.
   C I turn to fast food on rare occasions, and when I do, I stick with the salad and grilled chicken sandwich.

4. How often do you snack after 7:30 P.M.?
   A Nearly every night.
   B Only when I'm at the movies and want to reward myself with some popcorn.
   C Rarely, if ever.

Scoring Key: If you chose **A** for any of the above questions, you may struggle with the strictness of the nutrition program. If you circled **B** two or more times, you may also find the program difficult. Turn to the section titled "The Ultimate Makeover Nutrition Preprogram" later in this chapter to start the Ultimate Body Plan preprogram. If you scored well on the fitness test, you may start the Ultimate Body Plan while completing the nutritional preprogram.

THE "I'M ON MY WAY TO THE ULTIMATE BODY" FITNESS PREPROGRAM

This plan will help you to get into shape and prepare you for the extreme program if you need to reach any of the fitness measures outlined in the earlier assessment. The following 14-day program will get you in great shape, but it won't overwhelm you. Complete the following routine four times a week. Complete the routine in a circuit, moving directly from one exercise into the next without a break, if possible. Cycle through the entire routine two to three times, taking as little rest as possible and totaling about 30 minutes of continuous exercise.

1. CARDIO SCULPTING

Do…

- ONE MINUTE OF JUMPING JACKS WHILE HOLDING THREE-POUND DUMBBELLS.
- ONE MINUTE OF CROSSOVER PUNCHES WHILE HOLDING THREE-POUND DUMB-BELLS. To do a crossover punch, grasp a dumbbell in each hand. Stand with your abs tight and your back flat. Punch your left fist out diagonally, ending at torso level in front of your right ribs, completing a crossover punch. Pull back as you bend your knees, as if you were ducking an incoming punch. Repeat on the other side as you extend your legs, driving up from your heels and into your butt.
- ONE MINUTE OF UPPERCUT PUNCHES WHILE HOLDING THREE-POUND DUMB-BELLS. To do an uppercut punch, do the following: With your left elbow against your ribs and your knuckles turned up, punch upward,

as if you were punching someone in the jaw under the chin, trying to lift him off the ground. Pull back as you bend your knees, sitting back on your heels. Repeat with the other arm as you extend your legs.

- ONE MINUTE OF HOOK PUNCHES WHILE HOLDING THREE-POUND DUMBBELLS. To do a hook punch, lift your bent left arm so that it is parallel with the floor. Throw a hook punch, as if you were trying to hit someone on the side of the jaw. Pull back as you bend your knees, sitting back on your heels. Repeat on the other side as you extend your legs.

- 15 TO 20 SQUAT THRUSTS. Stand with your feet slightly wider than a hip's distance apart. Bend your knees, stick your butt back, and come into a squat. Continue to bend your knees as you bend forward from the hips, placing your palms against the floor under your breastbone. Press your hands into the floor as you jump and extend your legs behind your body, coming into a push-up position. Keep your abs tight the entire time. Recoil your legs and rise to the starting position.

- 30 SECONDS OF MOUNTAIN CLIMBERS. Start in a push-up position. Bend your right knee and jump it in, bringing your right thigh under the right side of your torso. Jump your right leg back as you simultaneously bend your left knee and jump it in. Continue alternating right and left.

2. PUSH-UPS

Complete 10 to 15 push-ups with your knees on the floor. (If you are strong enough, go ahead and try push-ups with your legs extended!) Position yourself with your palms on the floor under your chest, your back flat, your abs tight, and your knees, shins, and feet against the floor. Inhale as you bend your elbows and lower your chest toward the floor. Once you are hovering just above the floor, exhale as you push up to the starting position.

3. THE PLANK

Hold your body in a "plank" position, simulating the "up" part of a push-up for 30 seconds. Keep your abs tight and your back flat the entire time. Try to lengthen your entire body, reaching back through

your heels and forward through the top of your head. (Note: Once you are comfortable with the plank, try to do the same move with your hands placed on a medicine ball.)

4. DUMBBELL FLIES

Lie on your back on the floor. Grasp a dumbbell in each hand, extending your arms toward the ceiling above your chest. Bend your elbows and lower your arms out to the sides. Exhale as you press your arms back together, as if you were hugging a large oak tree. Complete 15 to 20 repetitions.

5. TRICEPS SKULL CRUSHERS

Lie on your back on the floor. Grasp a dumbbell in your right hand and extend your right arm toward the ceiling. Bend your right elbow as you lower your right hand toward the floor behind your head. Exhale as you raise your arm to the starting position. Complete 15 to 20 repetitions and then switch arms.

6. CRUNCHES

Lie on your back on the floor with your knees bent and feet flat on the floor. Place your fingertips behind your head. Draw your navel toward your spine, tuck in your tailbone, and exhale as you lift your shoulders. Inhale as you lower yourself. Complete 15 to 20 repetitions.

7. REVERSE CRUNCHES

Lie on your back. Extend your legs toward the ceiling, forming a 90 degree angle with your body. Exhale as you curl your tailbone up and in, scooping out your lower belly and reaching your feet toward the ceiling. Inhale as you lower yourself. Repeat 15 to 20 times.

8. BICEPS CURLS

Stand with a dumbbell in each hand. Place your feet under your hips, bend your knees slightly, and tighten your abs. Exhale as you curl the dumbbells toward your upper arms, keeping your elbows in close to your ribs. Lower as you inhale. Repeat 15 to 20 times.

9. LATERAL RAISES

Stand with a dumbbell in each hand. Place your feet under your hips, bend your knees slightly, and tighten your abs. Exhale as you raise your arms out to your sides to shoulder height. Inhale as you lower them to the starting position. Repeat 15 to 20 times.

10. FRONT RAISES

Stand with a dumbbell in each hand. Place your feet under your hips, bend your knees slightly, and tighten your abs. Exhale as you raise your arms in front to shoulder height. Inhale as you lower them to the starting position. Repeat 15 to 20 times.

11. LUNGES

Stand with your feet under your hips. Take a large step forward with your right foot. Sink down into a lunge, forming right angles with both legs. Exhale as you push back to the starting position. Then step forward and lunge with your left leg. Continue alternating right and left for 10 to 15 total repetitions.

12. SQUATS

Stand with your feet under your hips. Extend your arms in front for balance. Bend your knees and stick your butt out, stopping once your knees bend 45 to 90 degrees. Rise by driving up through your heels. Repeat 10 to 15 times.

13. PLIÉ SQUATS

Stand with your feet slightly wider than hip's distance apart. Turn your toes out and your heels in. Bring your body weight back onto your heels as you bend your knees and squat down while pushing your butt out. Exhale as you rise to the starting position. Repeat 10 to 15 times.

THE ULTIMATE MAKEOVER
NUTRITION PREPROGRAM

This preprogram will help you to take steps toward the Ultimate Body Nutrition Plan, allowing you to slowly adjust to the changes you will be making in your diet. If you scored well in the fitness test but need some time adjusting to the nutrition component of the plan, you can take some smaller steps toward the full nutrition plan by breaking it down into two phases.

Week 1 During the first week, ease yourself into eating regularly and preparing most of your meals. Give up fast food this week, and begin to create time to cook and brown-bag your lunch. I also want you to give up soda and fruit juice, including diet varieties. Instead, switch to herbal tea or club soda with a lime or lemon. Finally, get in the habit of eating regular meals, including three main meals and two small snacks. If you're a breakfast skipper, get into the habit of eating breakfast before you start the main program.

Week 2 In the second week, start to transition your diet away from processed foods (anything that comes in a box, can, bag, or shrink-wrap) and toward whole foods. I want you eating clean and green. Eat as many vegetables as you can. Switch from fatty sources of protein to lean sources of protein. For example, instead of having T-bone steak, opt for skinless chicken breast. For grains, choose whole grain options such as quinoa and brown rice over pasta and white rice.

THE SIX ULTIMATE STRATEGIES FOR SUCCESS

1. The next time you pack or buy a lunch, make it full of vegetables and whole foods.
2. When you're choosing protein, stick to the stuff that swims or flies (fish or poultry).
3. Keep your brain engaged when working out. Use your brain to feel each muscle contract and relax. Put your brain "in" whatever part of your body you are working at any given moment.

---

4. When designing your meals, *keep it lean and green*—pair a lean protein source with a vegetable.

5. Exercise every chance you get by using stairs instead of the elevator and avoiding escalators and moving walkways. When you are ready, try walking up two stairs at a time to really work your butt and thighs. Jogging up and down stairs is more challenging than working out on an exercise machine.

6. Whenever you cheat or backslide on the program, punish yourself with 25 push-ups and 15 lunges.

2
ULTIMATE MOTIVATION

For as far back as I can remember, my mother has told me that I was born with a special gift. I didn't always understand what she meant or what that gift was. At the ripe old age of 43 I finally think I get it. I believe I was born with the ability to inspire and motivate people. I have found that by living a sound life—physically, mentally, and spiritually—people often find a deep source of motivation. As I continue to grow as an individual, I understand the increasing importance and the delicate balance of staying motivated while living my life a way that engenders motivation in others.

Motivation, as I understand it, is the drive to succeed above all obstacles and the willingness to challenge oneself to rise above the fray. When mediocre and average won't do, your motivation will take you the rest of the way. Although I feel that I was born with it, don't fret. You can (as I did) nurture, foster, and develop a strong sense of motivation at any time in your life. This chapter will show you how to do just that.

You'll need to develop this motivation *before* you start on the 14-day Ultimate New York Body Plan. Too often, people underestimate the importance of mental readiness when starting a fitness and eating program. You'll need a strong exercise commitment—an hour to an hour and a half of exercise on most days. As I've mentioned, The Ultimate New York Body Plan combines a mixture of cardio sculpting and lightweight and high-repetition resistance training. You will use lightweight dumbbells, a stability ball, a medicine ball, and your own body weight to perform the exercises. The nutrition component of the program is definitely a little more extreme than the six-week program I outlined in *Sound Mind, Sound Body*. You will minimize calorie consumption and maximize fat and calorie burning. To accomplish this task, you must strictly adhere to my A, B, C, D, E, and F of nutrition outlined in Chapter 4, which basically means no alcohol, bread, starchy carbohydrates, dairy products, extra sweets, fruit, and most fats.

It takes commitment, motivation, strength, and stamina to pull all this off. The decision to do the Ultimate Body Plan is a decision to change your life. You're going to sweat, and you're going to challenge your body as you never have before. It's like that old adage I heard growing up—you must learn to walk, then run. In wellness, there are no shortcuts, no quick pills or potions that will bring about instantaneous results. To get the maximum benefit from this program, you will have to reach deep down and find the drive, determination, and motivation that will take you to successful completion.

You will need to engage your mind and your body in a way that will ensure success over the course of the next two weeks and will also help you maintain and improve upon those results beyond the two weeks. The strength, perseverance, and motivation you draw on will carry you through to the end, in the same way that these elements contribute to successfully running a marathon. Once you are committed to the task at hand, there is no backing down or turning back. Every mile brings you closer to realizing that precious goal. Once the goal is realized, all the training miles, aches, pains, and sacrifice seem worth it.

It's the same with every difficult task you take on in life, including this makeover program. You must firmly commit yourself to the process from the very beginning—no ifs, ands, or buts. Finding an hour and a half to exercise each day is a lot of time. You will feel tired on some days. You may feel sore. Nonetheless, you simply cannot skip a day or mindlessly go through the motions. The same goes for the Ultimate Body nutrition plan. You may have some days when you find yourself absolutely craving a bagel or a piece of buttered toast. If your commitment is firm, you'll be able to resist such temptations.

I like to think of this two-week process as a program that helps addiction-proof your body. Think of your affinity for bread, sweets, and other carbohydrates the same way you would an addiction to drugs, alcohol, or nicotine. You can kick any addictive habit with a firm, strong commitment and a high dose of motivation. The next 14 days will be tough. Some days may feel harder than others. Know, however, that it gets easier over time. As with any addiction, your food cravings will diminish. As your body gets into top shape, the soreness and fatigue will give way to a deep reservoir of energy and confidence. You'll find, as many of my clients have, that after 14 days you'll no longer feel the urge to eat bread or bagels or cheese or potato chips. After 14 days you'll begin to look forward to your workouts. So think of it as a boot camp, a temporary hurdle that leads to living fit and healthy for the rest of your life. You can do it. I believe in you.

I'll never forget the fitness trip I took to Capri, Italy. It was an exotic, but equally physically strenuous version of this program. The clients who accompanied me on the trip trained throughout the day—doing yoga, cardiovascular exercise, and strength training, among other things. I subjected them to pretty stringent nutritional guidelines as well. By the end of the trip, however, instead of craving pasta and biscotti, we were reaching for the protein and fresh grilled vegetables. We had trained, disciplined, and honed our bodies in such a way that "polluting" them with junk food (even Italian junk food) seemed sinful. Our bodies had indeed become our temples, and despoiling them would've been sacrilegious.

To help you cement your motivation and commitment, in this chapter you'll tackle seven crucial preparatory tasks. It's essential that you read this chapter and complete these tasks *before* you start the program. Although these mental toughness exercises will not sculpt your legs, butt, and tummy, they will help you to stick with the Ultimate Body Plan without cheating or backsliding. Just as importantly, these exercises will help you maintain your body makeover and translate the positive effects and benefits well beyond the two-week period and into your everyday life. The Ultimate New York Body Plan is life-transforming. The mental, physical, and spiritual all work in concert to bring about real, meaningful, and lasting changes. Without a solid approach to carry you beyond the first two weeks, how can anyone expect you to maintain your inspirational results?

STEP 1
FIND YOUR
TRUE SOURCE OF MOTIVATION

Incentive, inspiration, drive, enthusiasm, impetus, stimulus, spur, impulse, and driving force are just some of the synonyms I found when I looked up the word *motivation* in the dictionary. One of the prerequisites to successfully completing any challenge is motivation. Without it, any challenge, including this one, will ultimately become too daunting to see to completion.

Whether the "Extreme Makeover" women, one of my Victoria's Secret models, or you, the challenge is the same. We all need to find that special something that takes us beyond the ordinary. We must soar—not merely sail. At the risk of sounding too clichéd, I can't stress strongly enough the importance of striving to be the best that *you* can be. Such traits will follow you throughout this challenging program and won't desert you when the going truly gets tough.

The trick is to find and identify a challenge—something that evokes passion and meaning in your life. It is important to identify whether you are motivated for a cause, such as getting ready for a high school reunion or your wedding, or whether you are self-motivated and interested mostly in self-betterment. I caution you, however, against setting your sights on a particular number on the scale. On this program, you will exchange fat for muscle. Many of my clients have lost stunning amounts of fat, but their weight didn't drop quite so dramatically on the scale. Muscle weighs more than fat. It's also more compact and powers your metabolism. Each pound of muscle you build burns an additional 35 to 50 calories a day just to maintain itself. So even if your weight remains stable on the scale, exchanging a few pounds of fat for a few pounds of muscle will result in a slimmer, firmer, sexier body! Over the course of the two weeks, you will be transforming your body into a more efficient fat-burning machine. This will result in your body's ability to maintain your new self.

Of course, you may initially have decided to tackle the two-week Ultimate Body Plan because you wanted to look great in a swimsuit or stun your high school buddies at your next reunion. To uncover the true source of your motivation, however, look a little deeper. The pride found from looking great in a swimsuit pales in comparison to the pride and confidence gained from successfully completing the program without cheating or backsliding. Then, just imagine how confident and successful you can become when you maintain your results.

To find the true source of your motivation, contemplate the following questions:

❶ Why am I taking this makeover challenge?

❷ What do I hope to accomplish in 14 days?

❸ What do I hope to discover about myself during the next 14 days?

❹ What mental and spiritual strengths do I hope to build upon during the next 14 days?

Those last two questions may seem out of left field to you at this point. You may be thinking, "I want to look great in a swimsuit. What does that have to do with discovering something about myself?" Let me explain: Sculpting an amazing butt is quite motivational, but the loftier goal is finding your "soul light," the place inside you that, once lit, will guide you through your toughest travails. I have said it countless times—to all my clients at one point or another: "It's not just about a perky butt!" Unlocking and finding that place that we all have inside us is the secret to transforming and maintaining amazing physical, mental, and spiritual results.

Inner peace is often hard to grasp but easy to recognize. Recently, I was running to meet friends for dinner. I had been writing and lost track of time. I was feeling particularly stressed and could not find a taxi. I found myself getting caught up in a New York moment—not very pretty—when a homeless person stopped me and asked me if I had any spare change. In that split second I realized that this was all happening for a reason. I reached into my wallet, and the smallest dollar denomination I had was $20. I had been out only five minutes, and I was freezing. This guy had been out all day and night. I gladly gave him the $20 and told him to find someplace to get warm. That small act of charity allowed me to reconnect with my soul and, in the process, release unwanted toxic energy and replace it with positive energy, which I could feel pulsing through my body.

My mother discovered her soul light and inspiration to exercise recently when she was admitted to a hospital for surgery. As she was being administered the intravenous drip, the nurse told her to breathe deeply and think of something calming. For my mom, that meant thinking of my aunt (her youngest sister), who had been her best friend and who had passed away 13 years earlier. Mom heard my late aunt tell her she was going to be fine, that it wasn't her time yet. With that pleasant thought, Mom drifted off peacefully and awakened from the surgery feeling a little groggy but full of positive energy.

Mom insisted on going home that day. When I visited her, she was full of life. I believe my mother had an epiphany that day on the operating table. If at 67 years of age she could find the strength, courage, and fortitude to rise above a little adversity (and pain), then it was time to rethink and reprioritize the things that were most important to her. We spent the day looking at pictures and reminiscing about old times and people who had touched us over the years. We'd done that many times in the past, but this time it was different. Rather than taking on a sad tone, the experience was positive and uplifting. Every experience and each person in those old pictures represented a time and a moment that was very special. Together those moments formed a lifetime of love, learning, and growth that strengthened and enriched us.

On the way home from my parents' house, I telephoned my mother and told her how proud I was of her strength and courage. Since that day, my mother has started eating better and has pledged to start exercising again. I have purchased her a new recumbent exercise bicycle and put her on my nutrition plan. This all started with the power of positive thought and energy.

As far as I'm concerned, the power of positive energy is one of the most important mental practices needed for success. You must be positive in order to tap into your soul. You must let go of fear and self-judgment. By doing so, you allow yourself to connect spiritually and emotionally in a way that forms a formidable one-two punch.

Being a graduate of The Ultimate New York Body Plan will give you the strength, courage, motivation, and determination to keep that soul light lit and to continue to challenge yourself throughout your life. Perhaps you will strive to do better in school, seek a better job, or maintain more stable personal relationships. If you follow your soul light, you will be guided down the correct path. You will soar to new heights, and you'll feel better as a person as a result. Oh, and you'll look fantastic, too.

THE TRUE SOURCE OF MOTIVATION

To persevere on The Ultimate New York Body Plan, start thinking like a marathon runner. When ticking off one mile after another, the runner doesn't think about the number of calories she's burning or the shrinking size of her thighs. Rather, her motivation comes from the physical sense of accomplishment in pushing herself to her limit and beyond. Her motivation comes not only from the bragging rights of successfully completing a marathon, but also from the deep sense of pride that bubbles up from the inside once she's faced her demons and persevered. Think of your Ultimate Body the same way. Yes, you will sculpt the best body of your dreams. Yet, rather than focus your mental satisfaction on physical appearances, discover the deep well of motivation that bubbles up from the inside when you commit yourself to a challenging program and stick with it. When you push yourself to your limits and beyond, you'll not only achieve the physical results you seek, but you'll also discover your inner strength, fortitude, and motivation.

STEP 2
BECOME COMFORTABLE WITH FAILURE

You may at first think that I'm contradicting myself. How can you motivate yourself to succeed when you allow yourself to fail?

People cheat when they are afraid to fail. Remember that biology final that stood between you and the perfect 4.0 semester? We've all been there, that place where things seem so impossible that cheating seems the only answer.

With respect to The Ultimate New York Body Plan, the challenge will be great and the need for motivation essential. Don't let your self-doubt demons take over and cause you to cheat and sabotage your success. Equally important is what I often call fear of success. In this instance, we are so overwhelmed by the prospect of success that we sabotage our program and cheat, either by not training properly or by bingeing on Oreos and choco-late milk. In either case, the result is the same. Cheating derails us, at least temporarily, and challenges our ability to remain motivated.

Some clients whom I train are ultimately afraid of success and what that might mean for them. Are you hiding behind your weight? Is it your crutch or the excuse for why you haven't gotten that job, found the perfect date, and so on? Failure in and of itself isn't necessarily a bad thing. If you understand why you've failed in the past, you can prevent failure from recurring. By transforming yourself from the inside out, you will gain the strength and the courage to look failure dead on and say, "No more failure." You will be able to say that your life will be about achieving positive results. You will have the strength, courage, and added knowledge to persevere.

Often, the strongest offense is a good defense. Here are some tips for dealing with these fear-induced demons:

- RECOGNIZE AND UNDERSTAND YOUR FEARS. Think back to past attempts at weight loss, fitness, or good nutrition. Why did you cheat? What led you to overeat, underexercise, or generally not stick with your plan? Contemplating such questions will help you to cut future problems off at the pass. None of us is perfect. Look at past failures as opportuni-ties to learn more about yourself and propel yourself to future success.

- CONVINCE YOURSELF THAT FAILURE IS NOT AN OPTION. You will succeed! Yes, The Ultimate New York Body Plan is a physically and mentally chal-lenging program, but as long as you devote the proper amount of time and energy to it, you'll be able to accomplish your goals during the next 14 days.

■ CONTEMPLATE HOW HEALTHFUL EATING, REGULAR EXERCISE, AND WEIGHT LOSS WILL CHANGE YOUR LIFE. Examine your fears about weight loss and a healthful lifestyle. Do you worry, for example, that you no longer will be able to hang out at the bar with your friends? Will some people in your life work against your best efforts? When you face such questions head-on, you'll learn some valuable information not only about yourself and your priorities but also about your family and friends. Who is most important to you? Who truly supports you, and who does not? These are soul-searching questions. We all have certain people in our life who seem to come around only when we are needy or in trouble. They seem to relish the idea that we are less than perfect. Somehow they feel better about themselves if we fail.

TEST YOUR MOTIVATION

Answer the following questions to assess your inner motivation.

1. Have you ever made a New Year's resolution that involved getting in shape, starting a diet, or going to a gym, but you did not follow through?   Y   N

2. Have you ever gone on a diet but cheated or dropped out before achieving your goal?   Y   N

3. Do you have more than three different clothing sizes in your closet, corresponding to numerous weight gains and losses?   Y   N

Scoring Key: If you answered yes to any of these questions, make sure to complete every step in this chapter before embarking on The Ultimate New York Body Plan.

STEP 3
TAKE OWNERSHIP OF YOUR LIFE

We are all placed on this earth with a purpose and the ability to make choices in how to live, eat, and function from day to day. The choices we make affect not only us but also those around us.

You must recognize and accept that every action brings about a reaction, consequences that shape and form our everyday lives. Every moment in life is precious. Choose each moment of your life. Do you choose to sleep, be a couch potato in front of the television, or move? It's all your choice. If you stay in the moment and take ownership of your life and your choices, you will no longer be a passive victim. You will act, not react, with a positive attitude and a structured game plan. You will be the quarterback of your life and the architect of your future.

Keeping things "real" or manageable will make the most formidable task seem possible. Be mindful of each moment of each day. During your exercise sessions, keep your mind engaged. For example, by "placing your brain in your butt" while performing a lunge, you will ensure the perfectly proficient lunge. No longer will you be mindlessly lunging about, disconnected from what you are doing. Although physically challenging, working on a perkier butt will never seem daunting again.

Be just as mindful when you eat. This will save you from that bucket of popcorn in the movie theater, the basket of warm bread at the Italian restaurant, and the chocolate bar with almonds at midnight. I will never forget the time I was out with a friend at a restaurant in East Hampton. I ordered a salad. Everyone pretty much followed my lead, ordering big healthy salads and grilled vegetables. I was able to stare down the most tantalizing basket of warm, crusty bread. Not so for my friend, who quietly and quite methodically devoured the entire basket in just minutes. It could have been to soak up the three martinis he had downed like they were water. I watched in horror and complete disbelief as he unconsciously consumed hundreds of calories and a plethora of grams of empty carbohydrates. Had he stopped to think about what he was doing, he might have had one piece of bread, but he definitely would not have eaten the entire basket. Obviously, thinking about

Contract to Achieve My Ultimate Body

I _____ (your name) will be accountable and take responsibility for my actions and inactions. I will no longer let the past or any outside influences affect how I feel about or treat myself. A fight with my spouse or a difficult relationship with my family will not provide me with an excuse for eating a box of doughnuts. By entering into this pact with myself, I will immediately gain the power and control over my path.

I pledge to . . .

- Set aside one and a half hours a day for exercise

- Stick with the Ultimate Body Nutrition Plan for the next 14 days

- Follow the Ultimate Body Plan maintenance plan to maintain my results

- Push myself to my limits and beyond

- Stay in the moment when I exercise and eat

_____ (your signature)

what you are going to eat before you eat it will save you a lot of frustration, disappointment, heartache, and heartburn.

Taking ownership of your life starts today. The only person who can hold you accountable to this program is you. You can do it and stay the course! Do not start this program if anywhere in the back of your mind you think you might not give it your all. You must commit yourself 150 percent to success. Remember, this program is for you and about you, not about anyone else. Make sure your reasons for engaging in the program are pure and the focus is on you. No one else will be able to motivate you and get you through the rigors of The Ultimate New York Body Plan. Only once you make the 14-day program the top priority in your life—ahead of all other priorities for the next 14 days—will you be able to stick with the program without cheating or backsliding. I want you to try on that commitment. Choose what you will be giving up to make time for your exercise plan. Notice how attached you are to the foods you will be giving up. Your commitment must come from a deep place inside you. Be confident and be rock solid.

You must not only create time for your new habits but also firmly commit to the process. You are about to embark on a tough two-week journey. Once you commit to the process, you'll be able to navigate any stumbling blocks you meet along the way. Signing a contract with yourself is one way of cementing that commitment. It symbolically says to you that you've got both feet in the door.

STEP 4
STAY IN TOUCH WITH YOURSELF

Keeping track of your thoughts, feelings, and progress throughout the 14 days in a journal will help to keep you honest. It also may help you get through the toughest days, as expressing your thoughts and feelings on paper is often the best way to correct a problem.

I grew up with a father who kept journals about all his workouts. His journals, along with his collection of fitness magazines and periodicals, now serve as an ever-changing reference library and source for training inspiration. Even after the advent of computers, Palm Pilots, and a variety of other gadgets, Dad has remained true to his stenographer's pad and No. 2 pencil. He charts every set, repetition, and weight of every workout ever completed. He also notes the date and time of day, how he was feeling, and the overall objective of the workout. He also includes what he eats, including the quality and quantity of food and the time of day he ate it.

This may seem like an incredibly burdensome exercise (no pun intended), but the journal will help keep you focused on your goals and, at times, help you surmount any obstacles during the next two weeks. Your journal will also serve as a reference time and again.

In Chapter 5, you'll find space to jot down your thoughts and feelings during each day of the program. Use this space to write down your energy level, your daily nutritional consumption, your emotional and psychological energy and condition, and the time, duration, and intensity of your workout. The process of writing in the journal may take on a form of therapy for you. Be honest. Why you cheated on a specific day is just as important as how you cheated. In order to correct the problem, you must delve into it headfirst.

There are no hard-and-fast rules to writing in your journal, as long as you do it every day. Just allow the contents of your brain and your heart to spill out on the paper. Don't worry about grammar or spelling or penmanship. No one will read it but you. This daily diary will help you keep in touch with your inner world, helping you to uncover possible issues before they derail your success.

STEP 5
SCHEDULE YOUR EXERCISE TIME

Go get your day planner or Palm Pilot right now and, for each of the next 14 days, schedule your exercise time. Writing your exercise appointments in your agenda or calendar will help keep you from backsliding. Once you've written in your appointments and they are staring you in the face, you are less likely to "stand yourself up."

I recently completed the two-week program with Amy Larocca, an editor at *New York* magazine. She was very concerned about commencing the program because fashion week was just about to begin in New York City. As one of the leading editors of *New York* magazine, her time is rarely her own. This is exacerbated during fashion week when she is running from show to show with seconds to spare in between. I was confident that if we scheduled her workouts very methodically and had all of her food delivered to her door by 6:30 A.M., Amy would be well able to adhere to the rigors of the program.

My philosophy is about removing the obstacles that are placed (or that we unconsciously place) in our paths that take us out of our daily routine and prevent us from accomplishing our goals. Rather than burden Amy with entrées and salads and other cumbersome things, I packed her little sides of my Low-Fat Chicken Salad, pasta-free Turkey Lasagna, salmon burgers, and egg frittatas. By setting out a very specific game plan with Amy at the onset, we were able to get her through the insanity of New York fashion week and the intensity of my two-week Ultimate New York Body Plan. Seeing what she was able to accomplish during fashion week gave her the added confidence that she could maintain her amazing results after the program had ended.

Make exercise a ritual, like brushing your teeth. Do it at the same time every day, preferably first thing in the morning. Don't allow yourself to complete any other tasks until you have completed your exercise for the day. You can also use your calendar or day planner to chart your progress. You might check off tasks once you've completed them. Some of my clients like to draw smiley faces or place a star sticker in their day planner as a little motivational tool. You also might jot down foods as you eat them. You'll be less likely to deviate from the strict nutrition regimen if you are forced to memorialize your foibles.

STEP 6
GO SHOPPING

I always find buying new training shoes and clothes very motivating. It helps get my head set for the course charted ahead. What was better than those new shoes you bought in August just before the new school year began? I look back fondly on those times because the new shoes and new outfits served as promise and hope that the new school year would present new and exciting possibilities. I liken it to buying new composition or loose-leaf notebooks and putting the reinforcements on the pages (I know I'm dating myself) when you were in grade school. It helps get you in the mood. Here are a few things to stock up on before beginning the program.

- ■ SHOES. Purchase cross trainers that offer a good deal of arch and lateral support. Consult with a salesperson in a sporting goods store if you need guidance.

- ■ EXERCISE CLOTHING. Your clothes should be loose fitting and comfortable, but revealing enough that you can see what you are working on. For me, the more I see, the better—for example, I find looking at my legs when I work my legs both instructional and motivating.

- ■ MOTIVATIONAL MUSIC. Although I don't support extraneous things, such as music, because it can disconnect you from your mind-body connection, it's sometimes a necessary evil. Whether moving and soulful or heart-pumping and energizing, music is often that final something that puts it all in place.

- ■ MEDICINE BALL. You'll learn more about why you need a medicine ball in Chapter 3.

- ■ STABILITY BALL. The use of a stability ball and how to choose the correct size is also described in Chapter 3.

- ■ DUMBBELLS. You'll need lightweight dumbbells ranging from two to five pounds.

STEP 7
REDESIGN YOUR LIFE FOR SUCCESS

Where you live and where you work can either inspire you toward success or work against your best efforts. Before you start the program, you can take a few crucial steps toward making sure your living and work quarters do the former and not the latter. To change your current living and working situation to better prepare and support you throughout the program, do the following:

- Clean out your pantry of all processed foods, sweets, and other temptations and replace them with fresh foods, vegetables, and your favorite low-carbohydrate protein powder.

- If you're going to train in your house, designate an area that is exclusively yours and is to be used for exercise only. You can also do this in an apartment, hotel room, or office.

- Clear your work schedule of extraneous appointments, lunches, after-hours drinks, and dinners. It will be difficult to maintain the structure of the program in a restaurant.

- If possible, find a friend to do the program with you. You know what they say: Misery loves company! A training partner (when you find the right one) is helpful in motivating and pushing you to go beyond your preconceived notions of how much weight you can lift and how hard you can push yourself.

- Last but not least, sit down with your loved ones—significant other, children, parents, and/or best friends—and explain what you are about to embark on. This program is an incredibly challenging one, and you will find that having the proper infrastructure and support team will help get you through some of the more difficult times.

3

THE ULTIMATE NEW YORK BODY PLAN EXERCISE PROGRAM

During the past 15 years, I've worked with some of the most beautiful women in the world, and during that time they've made some pretty challenging requests that have run the gamut. If you've ever seen a Victoria's Secret fashion show, you'll see some of the results of the work that I've done with the likes of Heidi Klum, Naomi Campbell, and Bridget Hall. As their schedules are insanely busy, it is rare for the Victoria's Secret models to give me more than a couple of weeks to get them in lingerie shape and sculpt the type of body that looks fantastic when clad with just a few feathers and a pair of angel wings.

Yet, the most dramatic transformations I've seen have come from the many mere mortals I have had the pleasure and good fortune to work with. We mortals, although inspired by those beautiful angelic supermodels, have our own real-life issues. We have jobs, kids, husbands, wives, boyfriends and girlfriends, and so on. Being a mere mortal myself (with plenty of my own issues), I recognize and understand the challenges that we all face on a daily basis. There are bills to pay, jobs to do, and countless responsibilities to address. Often, the last thing on our minds is working out and following a strict nutritional regimen, but that's what it takes to sculpt the best body of your life.

What if I promised you that I have designed a program that will transform your life forever? I know you've heard this all before, but this time there are no smoke and mirrors and no gimmicks. My 14-day Ultimate New York Body Plan will give you the power, confidence, and tools you need to maintain your amazing results for the rest of your life. Let's face it, we all want to find that exercise and nutrition program that will take us past our plateaus and get us ready for bikini weather, the date, the reunion, and so on.

If you've read *Sound Mind, Sound Body*, then you already know that I ordinarily don't advocate these "get fit quick" schemes, because I feel they are often misleading, ineffective, and, once they're completed, leave you without the means to maintain whatever gains you have made. Before creating my 14-day Ultimate Body Plan, I thought long and hard about jumping into this area of fitness. I've worked hard to design a plan that not only will help you realize incredible physical changes (you can lose multiple dress sizes, pants sizes, inches, and percentages of body fat), but also will allow you to maintain your results and peace of mind.

You must incorporate the mental, spiritual, and emotional into all you do. The mantra "stay in the moment" will never ring truer than when you are grueling out workout after workout during the next 14 days. Indeed, you will need a great deal of motivation (see Chapter 2), along with some military-like willpower.

The Ultimate New York Body Plan will help you incinerate a mind-boggling amount of calories every day. Although results will vary from individual to individual, you should be able to burn up to 1,500 to 2,000 calories per day. At that rate, your body will function in caloric deficit mode, resulting in greater fat and weight loss. You will be a fat-burning, body-sculpting machine. Think Ferrari Testarossa! You'll improve your body's muscle-to-fat ratio, which, in turn, will speed up your metabolism, encouraging your body to burn fuel faster throughout the day, even when you're asleep.

Many people try to look great on no exercise or are misled by would-be experts into thinking that just a little bit of moderate exercise will do the trick. Guess what—they're wrong! To get results, you must work hard. If you lose weight through diet alone, your weight loss comes mostly from muscle tissue, not from fat tissue. This slows your metabolism, making weight gain more likely and future weight loss more difficult. Also, to truly look great, you must sculpt your muscles, and only exercise can do that. Think of yourself as a sculptor working on a beautiful statue. You need the raw clay, but you also need the tools to shape and mold it.

The workouts you will complete over the next 14 days—the very same ones that I used for my "Extreme Makeover" women and many others—are the most effective and efficient workouts around. To see results, however, you must commit to one to one and a half hours of exercise a day. Not 10 minutes, not 30 minutes, not 45 minutes. You will be devoting a full hour to an hour and a half a day toward sweat-inducing, body-transforming work-outs. That's what it's going to take to blast through a plateau, to lose those last five pounds, and to sculpt the best body in your life.

Cutting short or skipping just one exercise session or deviating from the nutrition plan can seriously endanger your results, so you must head into this program firmly committed. In fact, before you go any further, I'd like you to take out your Palm Pilot or day planner (or if you're like my dad, a notepad and No. 2 pencil) and schedule your exercise time. Make it your priority. Make exercise ritualistic, like brushing your teeth. That way, you'll be likely to show up every day.

THE PHILOSOPHY BEHIND THE PROGRAM

My routines include the most effective moves for burning fat and sculpting your body. Some of these moves are seriously challenging. None of them is a walk in the park. You will feel your heart pounding, your muscles stinging, and your fat cells burning. To sculpt the best body of your life in 14 days, you must push yourself to your limits and beyond. In the process of completing this program, you will constantly be redefining what your limits are. You have learned or will learn how to push those limits and, at the same time, incorporate my sound training philosophy. These are extreme workouts for ultimate results.

For the next 14 days, you will work out every single day. I know what you're thinking: "Don't I need rest for my muscles to recover?" For every rule, there are often exceptions. In this case, I have modified the traditional workout and adapted it to a 14-day format. In so doing, I will be challenging your body, but not injuring it. I've said it before and I'll say it again: This is an extreme program. Generally, I don't recommend that my clients work out every single day without a rest. Usually, I recommend they take one or two days off each week to catch up on life and to recuperate. This gives their muscles downtime. When you push your body to its limit, you tear down muscle tissue. That muscle tissue needs downtime in order to rebuild itself and become stronger. It's during your days off that satellite cells rush in to repair your muscle tissue, creating thicker and longer muscle fibers. If you go week after week without a break, your muscles become weaker, your immunity plummets, and your results take a nosedive. You may find that you even start gaining weight.

That's why I recommend you do this extreme program for just 14 days and no longer. After 14 days, you must insert rest days into your schedule to give your muscles and immune system time to rebuild and regenerate.

I also usually recommend that my clients rest for 48 hours between strength sessions. In other words, if they work their upper body on a Monday, they can work their lower body on Tuesday but can't address their upper body again until Wednesday. This again allows time for muscle tissue to be repaired and rebuilt. On my Ultimate New York Body Plan, however, you will target some muscle groups two days in a row. I accomplish this by dissecting each body part into several different zones. For example, the crossover lunges in the cardio sculpting routine attack the legs and the butt in a different way from prone scissors in the leg and butt toning routine. In addition, you'll target only the larger muscles multiple days in a row. In this program I pay particular attention to legs, butt, abdominals, and shoulders—the spots my clients ask me over and over again to help them sculpt, firm, and slim down.

Because you will be doing a high number of repetitions at a very light resistance, you will not tear down your muscles as you would during a traditional weight lifting session with heavy resistance. In fact, that's the goal of this program. We're not trying to build huge muscles; rather we're trying to sculpt, shape, and condition the muscle tissue you already have. Rather than tearing down muscle, you will stimulate your body into burning fat at a higher and more efficient rate. With the light resistance recommended in this program, your muscles should be able to recover from each session within 24 hours.

As I mention in Chapter 1, this is not a program for fitness beginners or for the faint of heart. You should be somewhat fit before you begin the core program. Ideally, you've already been exercising for six months and, possibly, have already completed the six-week program covered in *Sound Mind, Sound Body*. You are capable of doing 45 minutes of cardio along with regular strength or toning workouts. In addition, many of the exercises will be performed on or using a stability ball, requiring you to have some core strength and balance. I would definitely recommend working with a stability ball and getting comfortable with balancing on one before setting out on the program. See Chapter 1 to find out how to ready your body for this program.

YOUR DAILY SCHEDULE

For the next 14 days, you will work out every day, according to the following schedule:

You'll perform the 45-minute cardio sculpting routine coupled with 45 minutes of approved cardio (a total exercise time of one and a half hours) three days the first week and four the second. The core of the Ultimate New York Body Plan, my 45-minute cardio sculpting workout, includes 35 exercises done in sequence at a high intensity. It's a unique heart-pumping, sweat-inducing calorie and fat incinerator.

I have used versions of this cardio sculpting routine with great results on all my clients at one time or another. With Heidi Klum, the focus is usually on her hips, butt, thighs, and lower abdominals. The cardio sculpting routine I designed for her accentuates and improves upon the positives (and there are many). Believe it or not, her body is pear-shaped and, consequently, requires exercises that focus on the outer and inner thighs, butt, and lower abdominals, such as sumo lunges with side kicks and plié squats. Liv Tyler, on the other hand, is a classic apple and carries more weight in her torso. She has beautiful, shapely, sexy legs. As I was putting the finishing touches on this book, I was returning from Los Angeles where I was working with Liv to get her ready for the red carpet and presenting at the Academy Awards. Our focus was of course full body cardio sculpting with a special emphasis placed on her upper back, shoulders, and arms. As a general rule, Liv's cardio sculpting focuses on exercises that elongate, strengthen, and tone the muscles in her torso, arms, and abdominals such as dumbbell wraparounds and crunches with the medicine ball. As I do the final editing for this book, I have found out that Liv and her husband Roy are expecting their first child. Being young, healthy, and in good shape, Liv's workout routine should not alter much. The objective here will be to maintain her stamina and strength and keep her beautiful curves while keeping the weight gain (which is to be expected) to a healthy minimum. Because Liv is determined (as Heidi was) to stay healthy and active during the pregnancy, getting her back into shape postpregnancy should be relatively painless.

As I'm sure I will have my share of apples and pears reading this book and doing this program, I have included and incorporated both principles into the Ultimate New York Body Plan cardio sculpting workout. Consequently, you'll strengthen and tone muscles while simultaneously incinerating body fat. You can either do your cardio and cardio sculpting workouts in one long hour-and-a-half session or split them up, doing one in the morning and the other in the afternoon or evening. Pick the method that best fits into your schedule. Ideally, I would prefer that you do one or both programs first thing in the morning on an empty stomach, because this will maximize fat burning and set your metabolism rocking throughout the day. Having said that, don't use your inability to do it in the morning as an excuse to not do it at all.

For four days a week during week 1 and three days a week during week 2, you'll perform either (1) a 15-minute leg and butt routine coupled with 45 minutes of cardio or (2) a 15-minute abdomen, core, and back routine coupled with 45 minutes of cardio. (Consult "Your Ultimate Body Calendar" later in this chapter or the planner in Chapter 5 to learn which workouts to do on which days.) Unlike the cardio sculpting workout, your leg and abdominal routines will shape and tone your trouble spots with low-intensity sessions, zeroing in on and isolating your inner thighs, outer thighs, hips, buttocks, lower abs, waistline, and tummy. This series of incredibly effective exercises will help you to sculpt the sinewy, shapely muscles of a dancer or model. The philosophy is simple: You must use a low weight and high number of repetitions, and you must perform specific movements that focus on specific muscle fibers of each muscle group. Whereas the moves in the cardio sculpting routine work more than one muscle group at a time, these toning moves will zero in on specific spots on your body, adding shape and definition. I am not saying you can "spot lose," but you can spot shape, tone, and sculpt your way to a better body. Remember, you're a sculptor, and your body is the raw clay.

In addition to your cardio sculpting, legs, and abs workouts, you will also find a suggested warm-up and cooldown sequence. Although your warm-up and cooldown do not incinerate calories or sculpt your muscles, they are very important to your success. Your warm-up will help your heart to gradually speed up, easing you into your session. It will also gradually increase blood circulation to your muscles, reducing the risk of straining a muscle during your session. Your cooldown includes important stretches designed not only to help you stay limber but also to elongate your muscles. Do your warm-up before all your sessions and your cooldown afterward.

Altogether, you will work every muscle in your body, sculpting long, sexy, toned, firm muscles. Many people focus on just one area of their bodies, such as their thighs or butt, and ignore the rest. This doesn't help you get results. This creates an asymmetrical look—a toned butt but flabby arms, for example. There is nothing more beautiful than a symmetrical body where all the muscles are equally firm. My program will help you develop that very look. You'll create a flowing line of physical symmetry.

These total body workouts will also help correct muscle imbalances. Many people are stronger on one side of their body than the other. The equipment you'll use in this program will help counteract those muscle imbalances by forcing you to use your weak muscles as well as your strong muscles.

YOUR ULTIMATE BODY CALENDAR

Log the following workouts into your planner for the next 14 days.

WEEK 1

MONDAY
Cardio sculpting 45 minutes
Cardio 45 minutes

TUESDAY
Abs/core routine 15 minutes
Cardio 45 minutes

WEDNESDAY
Cardio sculpting 45 minutes
Cardio 45 minutes

THURSDAY
Legs/butt routine 15 minutes
Cardio 45 minutes

FRIDAY
Abs/core routine 15 minutes
Cardio 45 minutes

SATURDAY
Cardio sculpting 45 minutes
Cardio 45 minutes

SUNDAY
Legs/butt routine 15 minutes
Cardio 45 minutes

WEEK 2

MONDAY
Cardio sculpting 45 minutes
Cardio 45 minutes

TUESDAY
Abs/core routine 15 minutes
Cardio 45 minutes

WEDNESDAY
Cardio sculpting 45 minutes
Cardio 45 minutes

THURSDAY
Legs/butt routine 15 minutes
Cardio 45 minutes

FRIDAY
Cardio sculpting 45 minutes
Cardio 45 minutes

SATURDAY
Abs/core routine 15 minutes
Cardio 45 minutes

SUNDAY
Cardio sculpting 45 minutes
Cardio 45 minutes

THE CARDIO SCULPTING REVOLUTION

At the core of the Ultimate New York Body Plan is the 45-minute cardio sculpting workout that you will perform three days the first week and four days the second week. I developed this fitness method to strengthen and tone muscles while simultaneously incinerating body fat. A combination of high-intensity aerobic exercise and muscle toning moves, cardio sculpting keeps your heart rate up for 45 minutes.

I often speak of Heidi Klum and all the work we've done together. There's another beauty that I have had the good fortune to work with and help transform—Linda Evangelista. Linda is a modeling icon and is as beautiful now as when I first saw her grace the runway and numerous magazine covers around the world in the 1980s. She has embraced my cardio sculpting philosophy. All one has to do is open any major fashion magazine to realize that she has and continues to be in a class by herself. She has destroyed the notion that women modeling in their thirties cannot compete and, quite literally, hold their own. Linda is often forced to train on the road and on the run. Often her workouts are reduced to quick cardio sculpting sessions performed in ill-equipped hotel gyms or hotel suites (much like the ones you may be forced to use). Substituting sturdy chairs and the end of a bed for the traditional workout bench or stability ball is not uncommon. The beauty of the following program is that she (and you) will be able to perform these routines anywhere, at any time! One of the strongest principles I adhere to is the importance of the "no excuse workout."

The 45-minute cardio sculpting workout includes the following unique features:

- COMBINATION MOVEMENTS The use of combination movements is probably the most distinctive feature of this and many of my routines. Throughout the workout, you'll see that you often perform two movements at once. I might combine a jumping jack with a lateral raise or shoulder press, for example. This allows you to target your arms, abs, and/or legs at the same time, creating an efficient workout. Working so many muscle groups at once will help to keep your heart rate up, so that you burn fat as you shape your muscle. Also, doing two movements at once takes concentration. It's like walking and chewing gum or rubbing your belly while patting your head. It's hard to daydream, which helps you to zero in on exactly what you are doing and make every movement count.

- ■ SIGNATURE MOVES My signature moves, such as the frog jump, dumbbell wraparound, and sumo lunge with side kick, will help you build the muscle mass needed to permanently boost your metabolism after your workout while simultaneously burning between 400 and 600 calories during your workout. No other fitness method can produce such impressive results so quickly. These moves are unlike anything you have tried before. They are challenging, unique, and, most important, fun. They will keep you from getting bored—that's for sure. I've tweaked and developed these exercises over the years in response to the needs of my clients. Many of these moves use your body weight as resistance, making them perfect for when you are traveling.

- ■ HIGH REPETITIONS, LOW WEIGHT Other fitness programs encourage you to lift heavy weights and perform only 8 to 12 repetitions of each exercise. This works great for guys and girls who want to put on size (just think of Michel before we transformed her body). It's not the best program for women, however, who want sleek, sexy muscles. To sculpt your muscles without adding bulk, you must do a relatively high number of repetitions (about 15 to 20 per exercise) at a relatively low weight (using no heavier than five-pound dumbbells in some instances) while focusing on form and technique.

EQUIPMENT

In this program, you will need three pieces of equipment—the stability ball, dumbbells, and the medicine ball—all designed to help you to get the most out of your workouts. Each will force you to use the core muscles in your abdomen, sides, and back as you isolate other muscles. That way you will always be working at least two muscle groups at once—for a very effective, efficient workout. The following pieces of equipment are also convenient. You can store them under the bed or in a closet and take them out when you need them. That will encourage you to stick with the program. Here is what you will need.

Stability Ball

The stability ball—a vinyl, air-filled ball—can revolutionize your workout. These balls were first used, many years ago, in physical therapy sessions, helping patients recover from everything from back pain to neurological problems. The unstable surface of the ball forces you to recruit numerous muscles throughout your body to keep yourself balanced. Research shows that the ball can make just about any exercise more effective. In one study, for example, people who did crunches while seated on a ball recruited more muscle fibers in their abdominals than those who did crunches on the floor. Here's how it works: Let's say you lie on the ball as if it were a bench and perform a traditional chest press. You'll strengthen your chest muscles as you press the dumbbells away from you. You'll also firm your thigh and butt muscles as they keep your hips in position. Finally, you'll tone your abdomen as it works to keep you balanced on the ball. How's that for a total body workout?

There are now more fitness ball manufacturers than any reasonable human being can keep track of, from Gymnic to BodyTrends to Duraball. Look for a burst-resistant stability ball, and buy the right sized ball for your height.

BALL DIAMETER	HEIGHT
53 cm (21 in)	4 ft 11 in to 5 ft 4 in
65 cm (25 in)	5 ft 5 in to 5 ft 11 in
75 cm (29 in)	6 ft +

When you sit on the ball with your feet on the floor, your knees should bend at a 90-degree angle. Generally, that means ball sizes shown on the previous page work for the heights shown.

Dumbbells

You'll use lightweight dumbbells—ranging from two to five pounds (or higher if you are able)—to perform many of the exercises of the program. I like dumbbells because they support your mind-body connection. They allow you the mobility and flexibility you need to tweak an exercise to your body's specific needs. Dumbbells also encourage you to work both sides of your body equally. Most of us have a dominant side. For example, if you are right-handed, your right arm is your dominant arm, and it is probably stronger than your left. If you lifted a barbell with both hands all the time, your right arm would use more effort to lift the bar, to compensate for your weaker left. With dumbbells, however, your left arm must exert just as much effort as the right. Remember that this program contains numerous repetitions. Even though a five-pound dumbbell may seem light to you right now, it will feel very heavy after 20 repetitions. I recommend you start with two- or three-pound dumbbells and move up to five-pound dumbbells once (if ever) the workout feels too easy. Look for dumbbells with a soft coating, and buy them in a color you like. This way you're more likely to keep them out, and, with them in constant sight, you're more likely to use them.

Medicine Ball

New and improved versions of the old, heavy, leather ball you saw in your high school gym, today's medicine balls are covered in soft plastic and come in many colors and weights. The medicine ball adds fun and variety to training. You can use a medicine ball to strengthen any area of your body. It serves as a perfect complement to the stability ball. Medicine balls come in weights starting at just over two pounds and ending at 24 pounds. You'll want a ball that weighs between four and ten pounds. These balls are often weighted in kilograms. If they are, choose a ball that weighs between one and four kilograms.

CHOOSING
YOUR CARDIO

Your daily cardio session will help incinerate calories, condition your heart and lungs, and keep your mind focused on your goals. To make it most effective, you must choose a form of cardio that helps you get your heart rate up—I mean really up.

Many people choose walking as a form of cardio. That's fine for most programs, but if you want to sculpt the best body of your life in a relatively short period of time—and since you are reading this book, I'm assuming that you do—walking just isn't going to cut it. Every once in a while I'll see a true power walker out there, someone who is really pushing the pace hard, pumping his or her arms, and breathing hard. That's the exception to the rule. Most walkers daydream, look at the scenery, and generally walk at such a low intensity that they burn very few calories. On this program, walking simply doesn't get your heart rate up high enough to burn the number of calories you need to burn to see the fat loss that you want to see.

I feel the same way about the stationary bike. Most people get on the stationary bike and pedal away mindlessly as they listen to music or watch television. This just isn't going to cut it. Also, cycling tends to add bulk to the thighs, which is another reason why I don't recommend it.

When you do your cardio, I want you to feel out of breath. I want you to hear and feel your heart and breathing rate speed up. Every minute counts on this program, so you need to challenge yourself. That's why I suggest the following types of cardio, which either work the upper and lower body simultaneously or are just challenging enough to "push the envelope."

The Gauntlet

The gauntlet, a stair-climbing type of machine, looks and operates like an escalator. Vary the way you step, alternating between taking one and two steps at a time. When taking two steps at a time, you should feel as if you are lunging on the machine. Give your bottom leg a full stretch before stepping back up. When you're taking smaller steps, set the machine at a higher level (at least 10 or 11) and alternate in one- or two-minute intervals between the two-step and the one step.

ULTIMATE TIP: *Stick your butt out as you climb on the machine. This will shift the focus from your thighs and quadriceps to your butt and hips, shaping your problem spots. If you are coordinated and have good balance, you may also try something that I have recently added to my clients' routines. Instead of facing straight ahead, turn your body completely to the side and step your right leg over your left leg, alternating between one and two steps for 10 repetitions, then switching to the other side. This will give you an effect similar to crossover lunges, working across and below the butt. To engage the upper body (I'm sure you thought I forgot about that!), hold a pair of dumbbells and do either shoulder presses or dumbbell curls while stepping on the machine. Do not add the dumbbells unless you are (a) very coordinated and (b) proficient on the gauntlet.*

Rowing Machine

To get your heart rate up to the right level on a rowing machine, set the machine to a level of between 5 and 7. Do no less than 2,500 to 5,000 meters, which (if you're in good shape) should take from 10 to 30 minutes.

ULTIMATE TIP: *If you're rowing correctly, you will begin to feel a nice burn in the lower part of your butt—the part that hangs below the bathing suit if it is not toned up. Make sure to keep your brain down there and press through your heels as you extend your legs. In addition, make sure to keep your abdominals tight and to relax your trapezius muscles. The focus in your upper body should be in your middle and upper back— squeezing from the shoulder blades. For variety, you can alternate gripping the handles over- and underhand and pulling high and low into your torso.*

Elliptical Trainer

My favorite brand of elliptical trainer is the Cybex Arc Trainer. I like the motion and the way it engages the quadriceps, hips, and butt while taking stress out of your knees. As with the other cardiovascular machines, don't be concerned with setting the machine at too high a level, because you don't want to burn your muscles out. Rather you want to get your heart pumping. The goal here is to aim for time and endurance first and then intensity.

ULTIMATE TIP: *Sit back in your heels on this machine. I often see people positioning their torsos straight upright, which places too much emphasis on the quadriceps. Stick your butt out as much as possible since this will shift the focus into your butt, hamstrings, and outer thighs and out of your quadriceps. Please take this tip very seriously as it is probably the most common mistake I've seen on the elliptical machine. Remember, you don't want big, muscular thighs (unless you're considering the World's Strongest Person Competition and you're entering the squatting competition).*

Jump Rope

If you like to jump rope, work up to 30 minutes (or more if you can). If you can't skip rope continuously for that length of time, do intervals and add the following exercises to up the ante.

ULTIMATE TIP: *To stoke the cardio fires, alternate push-ups or jumping jacks with shoulder presses or frog jumps in between jump rope sets.*

Running

If running is your thing, make it count. No lazy sightseeing jogging, please. You do not have the luxury of lots of time on your hands. Vary your speed and, if possible, try to add a cross-country element to it if there are any hills around. Do no less than quarter-mile sprints at no less than 5.5 to 6.0 m.p.h. If you are unable to do this speed or duration, try another form of cardio more appropriate for your fitness level (elliptical machine, rowing machine, jump rope, or even jumping jacks with shoulder presses).

ULTIMATE TIP: *Make your run a little more challenging by running backward every once in a while. Of course, don't try this in traffic or where you may end up running into something or someone. You may also turn to your side and cross right foot over left and left foot over right. You may remember that drill from football, baseball, or field hockey practice. It's very challenging and very effective.*

MAKING THE BEST OF EACH WORKOUT

To get the most out of the Ultimate Body Plan exercise program, follow these pointers.

Use Your Mind Your mind is a powerful fitness tool. Most people train unconsciously, disengaging their minds as they work out. Although this may help you to work your way through a session when you don't really want to be there, it doesn't help you to reach your goals. Watching television, day-dreaming, or chatting with a friend as you exercise causes you to tune out the subtle yet important signals your body sends to you. When you fail to engage your mind, you simply go through the motions of an uninspired work-out that feels dull not only to your mind but also to your muscles. Once you engage your mind and feel every heartbeat and every muscle movement, you'll be able to squeeze out a few more reps and push yourself to the edge. Whereas an unengaged mind would have called it quits, you'll push yourself just a little bit harder. By staying engaged and "in the moment," you will be able to safely extend your edge, challenging yourself every step of the way. You'll be able to hone your form, increasing the effectiveness of every movement. And you'll be able to move with more power and energy. So take a tip from the yogis and bring your awareness inside your body throughout your sessions. Feel every movement, every breath, and every heartbeat. By staying in the moment, you will actually feel your muscle fibers changing, shaping, and elongating. Remember, you're a sculptor, and your body is the clay.

I recently had a moment with a female client who in my opinion was not getting the most out of her workout sessions. I had one of those necessary conversations and spoke to her about what I thought was happening and not happening in her daily training routines. During her cardiovascular sessions, which often lasted one hour, she definitely worked up a good sweat and was burning calories, but she wasn't losing the weight and seeing the results that I thought she should. Upon closer investigation I realized that she not only had a portable e-mail device with her, but she carried her cell phone, listened to music, and channel surfed on the television. How's that for disengaging and disconnecting from your inner voice? She was also bringing too much of her outside work and environmental stress onto the gym floor.

I told her, "There is a time and a place for everything, but to maximize the efficiency of the workouts, you'll need to check everything at the door!" Since giving her that advice, I have seen great improvement in her focus during our workout sessions, and she is down to holding just the remote control for the television during her cardio sessions. She is definitely on her way to more focused, efficient, and ultimately more effective workouts.

Feel the Work For each of the exercises in the program, I've suggested a number of repetitions (the number of times you repeat a specific movement) and sets (the number of times you repeat an exercise) to perform. However, I'd rather that you tap into your mind-body connection and discover the right number of reps and sets for your unique body and fitness level. No two people are built the same. Whereas 12 frog jumps might put one person on the couch for the rest of the day, they might do nothing for someone else. Also, how strong you feel on a Monday can change by Tuesday or Wednesday. You may need to do more or fewer reps or sets of various exercises based on how your body is responding that day.

To find the right number of reps and sets for you, listen to your body. Aim for healthy muscle exhaustion, working to your maximum perceived rate of exertion (MPRE). When you are done with a set, you should feel as if you've worked that muscle group to its limit. That might happen in 15 reps or 20. It doesn't matter how long it takes to get there, as long as you meet your challenge head on. The 45-minute cardio sculpting program is a cumulative one. Be mindful that although it may not seem very challenging in the beginning, your body will soon be cooking, your heart pumping, and your energy rocking. Remaining strong, focused, and steady will carry you through the program.

Keep Your Joints Soft When you're standing upright, never lock out your elbows or knees. Always keep them soft. That doesn't mean they should flop around like fish out of water. They should be slightly bent, yet firm and flexed. This will help you to work the muscles around your joints while protecting your joints. This is particularly important when you're doing jumping motions such as squat jumps, jumping lunges, frog jumps, and jumping jacks. Land on soft legs (knees), keeping your brain in your butt, and take the impact of the landing in your heels and drive it up through your hamstrings and throughout your legs. If, on the other hand, you stiff-leg your landing, you'll feel shock travel right into your joints—where you don't want it.

Use a Mirror Your first one or two runs through the routines may take a bit longer than prescribed. Depending on your familiarity with using a stability ball, it may take a little getting used to. I suggest you exercise in front of a mirror where you can watch your form. As you perform each movement, feel where the motion takes place in your body. Are you feeling it in the right place? If not, what changes can you make to your form to correct yourself? You might physically touch the muscle you wish to fire as you move. This helps you to subconsciously police your body mechanics and make small adjustments that increase your results. The mirror in this instance is not about vanity at all. Although some of us enjoy a good mirror look every now and again, make sure to check your form and engage the mind-body connection to ensure proper form and technique as you go on in the routine.

Do It Right I've said it before and I'll say it again: "Put your brain in your butt." I didn't make that up to sound kitschy or cute. Think about it when performing a lunge, and let it become your mantra. If you engage your mind and body simultaneously, you will perform the exercise correctly. That being said, I set forth very explicit descriptions of each and every movement and exercise in my 14-day Ultimate Body Plan. In life many things aren't necessarily black and white. However, when it comes to exercise form and technique, the only acceptable way to do a routine is my way, and that's the correct way. I have designed and tested this routine and the appropriate form for each exercise. When performing lunges, for example, you will anchor with your front heel, making sure not to let your knee go past your toes. By envisioning your heel anchoring the movement, it is easier to understand the power and the energy of the lunge driving up through your heel into your hamstrings, hips, and butt. Consequently, you will also know when your form is off and how to correct it.

You have only 14 days to sculpt the best body of your life. You need to do everything right. Proper posture is the foundation for every movement. The basic posture for every move you make will be the same. To learn it, stand and focus your attention on your tummy. Firm your abdomen and suck it inward. At the same time, firm your glutes (butt). When you do this, your pelvis should tilt back, flattening and supporting your lower back. Bring your body weight into your heels and away from the balls of your feet. Retract your shoulder blades and pull them close together, expanding your chest. Focus on your head, aligning it with your body and centering it above your shoulders.

Once you have it, close your eyes and feel it. Whether you are standing, sitting, or lying down, you will use this basic posture: shoulders back, abs and butt firm.

Stay Positive A client once told me that I looked like Yoda. I was amused and offended at the same time. After some reflection, however, I realized that Yoda and I share many of the same principles and beliefs. Yoda was a teacher. That was his passion. I, too, feel that passion. He believed in the power of positive energy. His instruction of "No try . . . do" resonates with me. I have implemented that mantra in my life and use it when training clients. Everything and anything is possible if we set our minds to it and we believe in our own invincibility. I'm not saying that this program is not challenging. Indeed, it may be the most physically and mentally demanding thing you've ever done. As you progress over the 14 days, however, you will feel yourself getting stronger and building up stamina and confidence that might have otherwise been impossible. Once you understand the power of positive thought, you will understand that the opposite—negative energy—will drain you of all good and keep you from succeeding with this program and in life.

Believe in Yourself These routines should feel challenging. You must work hard to build a great body. Don't feel depressed or upset with yourself if the moves challenge you. Keep your chin up. In two weeks you'll be stronger, slimmer, and firmer than you've been for quite some time (possibly even your entire life). As you prepare yourself to start this program, remember that the difference between success and failure isn't measured in inches, pounds, and percentages of body fat alone. In the quest for the perfect perky butt, don't lose sight of the ultimate prize—self-empowerment. Anything can be and is attainable.

Not all my clients are a size 2. Not everyone is meant to be that small. Remember, we are going to get you to realize your own personal best, not someone else's generic idea of your personal best.

ULTIMATE WARM-UP ROUTINE

The following sequence should take you three to five minutes to complete. Use it as a warm-up for your cardio sculpting routine, toning routines, or cardio workout. Your warm-up primes your heart, lungs, and working muscles, as well as your mind, for your workout. It slowly increases your heart rate and brings more blood to your working muscles, protecting them from sudden strains.

TOTAL BODY STRETCH

A. Stand with your feet under your hips. Reach your arms overhead and stretch up through your fingertips, lengthening your entire body.

B. Slightly relax the left side of your body, keeping your left arm overhead, as you reach up through your right fingertips. Then, slightly relax the right side of your body as you

reach up through your left fingertips. Continue alternating stretching your right and left side for 30 seconds.

LATERAL SIDE STRETCH

A. Stand with your feet under your hips. Reach your arms overhead and stretch up through your fingertips, lengthening your entire body.

B. Keeping your abs tight and chest open, stretch up and over to the left, lengthening the right side of your torso and feeling a stretch through your right ribs and back. Inhale as you rise. Then stretch up and over to the right, lengthening the left side of your body. Continue alternating left and right for 30 seconds.

INNER THIGH STRETCH

A. Stand with your legs in a wide angle, about a leg's length apart.

B. Bend your right knee and shift your body weight toward the right, placing your palms on your right thigh. Keep your left leg extended. Hold for 20 seconds. Rise to the starting position and repeat on the left side.

PLIÉ SQUAT WARM-UP

A. Stand with your legs in a wide angle, about a leg's length apart. Turn your toes out about 45 degrees and your heels in. Bend your knees and sink down into a squat. Tuck in your tailbone and bring your knees back (don't allow your knees to collapse forward).

B. With your torso upright, abs tight, and palms on your thighs, hold this position as you lift your left heel and come onto the ball of your left foot. Lower that heel and then lift your right heel. Alternate lifting your left and right heels for 30 seconds.

MEDICINE BALL ROTATION

A. Stand with your feet slightly wider than a hip's distance apart. Grasp a medicine ball with both hands, extending your arms from your chest.

B. Twist your torso to the right, keeping the ball extended from your chest. Return to the starting position, and then twist to the left. Continue alternating right and left for 30 seconds.

AROUND THE WORLD

A. Stand with your legs slightly wider than a hip's distance apart. Place a medicine ball just in front of and to the outside of your right foot. Bend forward from the hips, and grasp the ball with both hands near your foot.

B. Lift the ball in a half circle up the right side of your body, over your head, and down the left side of your body, until it rests on the floor near the outside of your left foot. Repeat a half circle to your right. Continue circling right and left, left and right for 30 seconds.

45-MINUTE CARDIO SCULPTING ROUTINE

Complete the following routine four times a week, according to the schedule provided in "Your Ultimate Body Calendar" earlier in this chapter. I've designed this routine with strategic rest breaks. You'll complete a series of heart-pounding movements and then a few strengthening movements that will allow your heart rate to slow down and recover. Then you'll speed up your heart rate yet again. Make it your goal to progress directly from one exercise into the next without stopping. In the beginning you may find that you need to catch your breath from time to time. As you progress in the program, however, try to minimize your rest breaks.

Some movements in this routine require a great deal of balance, coordination, endurance, and strength. Do not attempt this routine until after you have taken the fitness test in Chapter 1 and completed the fitness preprogram, if required. The fitness preprogram will build the balance, coordination, strength, and cardiovascular fitness you need to complete this routine safely.

BALL TAP

A. Stand with your feet under your hips and with your stability ball just behind you.

B. Bend your knees and squat down, sitting back onto the ball. Let your butt touch the ball, then press through your heels and rise to the starting position. Avoid using momentum by bouncing up off the ball. Repeat 20 to 30 times.

BALL TAP WITH MEDICINE BALL

A. Stand with your feet under your hips and with your stability ball just behind you. Grasp a medicine ball in both hands with your arms bent, holding the ball near your chest.

B. Bend your knees and squat down, sitting back onto the stability ball. Let your butt touch the ball, then press through your heels and rise to standing.

c. Press the medicine ball overhead as you extend your arms. Lower the ball to your chest. Repeat 20 to 30 times.

SIDE SQUAT WITH MEDICINE BALL WOOD CHOP

A. Stand with your feet slightly wider than a hip's distance apart. Grasp a medicine ball with both hands, holding the ball just above your right shoulder as if it were an axe that you were getting ready to swing.

B. Bend your left knee and lower yourself into a half squat, keeping the right leg extended. As you bend your knee, swing your axe (the medicine ball) in a diagonal wood-chopping motion, bringing the ball toward and just past your left knee. Rise to the starting position. Repeat 20 to 30 times to the left and then repeat on your right side.

JOGGING IN PLACE WITH MEDICINE BALL

A. Stand with your feet under your hips. Grasp a medicine ball with both hands. Extend your arms in front at chest level.

B. Jog in place for 30 seconds with the medicine ball extended at chest level. Do not put all your weight on your toes, as this will stress your knee joints. As always, I advise you to distribute your body weight in such a way as to minimize stress to the knees. In this case, I would advise you shift your body weight onto the balls of your feet.

C. Continue to jog in place as you rotate your torso to the left with your arms extended. Jog for an additional 30 seconds. Then rotate your torso to the right and jog for 30 seconds.

JUMPING JACKS WITH SHOULDER PRESS

A. Stand with your feet under your hips. Grasp a dumbbell in each hand with your elbows bent and hands at ear height.

B. Jump your feet out into a wide angle as you press the dumbbells overhead, keeping them above your shoulders. Bring your feet back together as you lower the dumbbells. Repeat 20 to 30 times.

JUMPING JACKS WITH LATERAL RAISES

A. Stand with your feet under your hips. Grasp a dumbbell in each hand, holding your hands at your sides with your palms facing in.

B. Jump your feet out into a wide angle as you raise your arms out to the sides to shoulder height with your palms facing and parallel to the floor. Bring your feet back together as you lower your arms. Repeat 20 to 30 times.

Shadow Boxing with Dumbbells

A. Grasp a dumbbell in each hand. Stand with your abs tight and your back flat. Punch your left fist out diagonally, ending at torso level in front of your right ribs, completing a crossover punch. Pull back as you bend your knees, as if you are ducking an incoming punch. Repeat on the other side as you extend your legs, driving up from your heels and into your butt. Repeat 20 to 30 times on each side.

B. With your left elbow against your ribs and your knuckles turned up, punch upward, as if you are punching someone in the jaw under the chin with an uppercut, trying to lift him off the ground. Pull back as you bend your knees, sitting back on your heels. Repeat with the other arm as you extend your legs. Repeat 20 to 30 times on each side.

C. Bring your bent left arm up so it is parallel with the floor. Throw a hook punch, as if you are trying to hit someone on the side of the jaw. Pull back as you bend your knees, sitting back on your heels. Repeat on the other side as you extend your legs. Repeat 20 to 30 times on each side.

Calf Raises with Dumbbell Presses

A. Stand with your feet under your hips. Grasp a dumbbell in each hand. Place your hands by your ears and your elbows out.

B. Lift your heels and rise onto the balls of your feet and simultaneously press the dumbbells straight overhead and back down to chest level. Lower and repeat 20 to 30 times.

Squat Thrusts with Medicine Ball

A. Stand with your feet slightly wider than a hip's distance apart. Grasp a medicine ball with both hands at chest level with your elbows bent.

B. Bend your knees, stick your butt back, and come into a squat.

C. Continue to bend your knees as you bend forward from the hips, placing the medicine ball on the floor under your breastbone.

D. Press your hands into the medicine ball as you jump and extend your legs behind your body, coming into a push-up position. Keep your abs tight the entire time. Recoil your legs and rise to the starting position. Repeat 10 to 15 times. During your last repetition, remain in the modified push-up position and proceed directly into mountain climbers.

MOUNTAIN CLIMBERS WITH MEDICINE BALL

A. From the push-up position in the squat thrust, bend your right knee and jump it in, bringing your right thigh under the right side of your torso.

B. Jump your right leg back as you simultaneously bend your left knee and jump it in. Continue alternating right and left for 15 to 30 seconds. Return to the squat thrusts, repeating for an additional set. Then return to the mountain climbers, repeating for an additional set, before moving on to the push-ups.

PUSH-UPS WITH STABILITY BALL

A. In addition to working your arms and chest, push-ups engage the abs and provide a nice transition into the following moves. You will super-set the push-ups, ball tuck, and pike together into a mini-routine.

Place your tummy on the stability ball and palms on the floor in front of the ball. Walk your hands forward as you slide your torso forward on the ball, until you come into a push-up position with your thighs, shins, or balls of your feet on the ball. (Note: Placing your thighs on the ball is the least challenging option, your shins slightly more challenging, and the balls of your feet or your toes the most challenging.) Place your palms on the floor under your chest. Make sure your abs are tight and back is flat. Do not allow your hips to sink downward.

B. Bend your elbows out to the sides as you bring your face and chest toward the floor. Exhale as you extend your elbows and push up to the starting position. Repeat 10 to 15 times. Remain in the push-up position and proceed directly to the ball tucks.

BALL TUCKS

A. From the push-up position, bend your knees and bring them in toward your chest.

B. Extend your legs as you push the ball back to the starting position. Keep your abs tight the entire time. Repeat 10 times.

C. Bring your knees in toward your right armpit. Extend your legs as you push the ball back to the starting position. Keep your abs tight the entire time. Repeat 10 times.

D. Bring your knees in toward your left armpit. Extend your legs as you push the ball back to the starting position. Keep your abs tight the entire time. Repeat 10 times. Remain in the push-up position and proceed to the pike.

PIKE

A. From a push-up position with the balls of your feet on the stability ball, raise your hips toward the ceiling as you bring the ball in toward your hands, keeping your abs tight and legs extending. Your torso should form an upside-down V shape. Hold 10 to 15 seconds.

B. Proceed back to the push-ups, repeating the push-ups, ball tuck, and pike one to two times.

PLATYPUS WALK WITH MEDICINE BALL

A. Grasp a medicine ball with both hands and extend your arms overhead. Squat in a sitting position with your knees aligned with your toes and your butt sticking back as far as you can get it.

B. Keep your core tight as you walk forward, pushing off through each heel. If you perform the move correctly, your butt and inner thighs will be on fire. Walk across the room in one direction and then reverse and walk backward. If your room is small, repeat crossing the room one time before moving on to jumping lunges.

JUMPING LUNGES

A. Stand with your feet under your hips. Take a large step forward with your right foot. Sink down into a lunge, forming right angles with both legs.

B. Spring upward, launching both feet off the floor, and switch positions with your legs so your left foot is in front and right leg behind. Land and sink down into another lunge. Alternate your legs 10 to 15 times on each side.

SIDE STEP SQUAT WITH MEDICINE BALL

A. Stand with your feet slightly wider than hip distance apart. Grasp a medicine ball in both hands at chest height, with your elbows bent.

B. Bend your left knee and lower yourself into a half squat, keeping the right leg extended. As you squat, press the ball away from your chest as you extend your arms, keeping your arms parallel to the ground. Hold for a count of 5. Rise and pull the ball back to your chest. Repeat 15 times and then switch sides.

LOW PLANK ON STABILITY BALL

Place the stability ball on the floor and walk out into a push-up position with the balls of your feet on the stability ball and your palms on the floor under your chest. Keep your abs tight and don't allow your hips to sag downward. Hold for 15 seconds.

HIGH PLANK ON STABILITY BALL

Come into a push-up position with your palms on the stability ball and balls of your feet on the floor. Your legs should be extended and your body should form a diagonal line from your heels to your head. Hold for 15 seconds. Return to the low plank and repeat the low plank and then the high plank one to two times.

PUSH-UPS TO T-STANDS

A. Come into a push-up position with your palms on the floor under your shoulders and the balls of your feet on the floor.

B. Lift your left leg a few inches off the floor. Bend your elbows out to the side as you lower your face and chest toward the floor. Once your face is hovering just above the floor, exhale as you push back up.

C. Rotate your torso to the left, placing your right leg and foot on top of your left and lifting your right arm toward the ceiling. You should now be balanced on your left palm and the outer edge of your left foot. Your abs should be tight, your tailbone slightly tucked, and your waist and your body straight, reaching up toward the ceiling. Hold this position for two seconds. Lower back into a push-up position, repeating a push-up with your right leg raised and then a T-stand with your left arm raised. Continue alternating legs and arms for a total of ten push-ups and five T-stands on each side.

SUMO LUNGE WITH SIDE KICK AND FROG JUMP

A. Stand in a "sumo" position with your feet slightly wider than a shoulder's distance apart, your knees bent, and your body weight over your heels.

B. Take a large step sideways with your right leg, bringing your right knee in toward your chest and then over to the right in one continuous motion.

C. As soon as your right foot touches the ground, bring your knee back into your chest and complete a side kick, kicking your right heel out to the side into the stomach of an imaginary opponent (or jaw if that imaginary person is height compromised).

D. Lower your right leg to the floor into the sumo position. Squat down while sticking your butt out. Keep your knees just above—not in front of—your toes.

E. Spring up while thrusting your arms overhead. Land on your heels, rolling forward onto your toes. Repeat with a sumo lunge and side kick with your left leg and another frog jump. Continue alternating right to left until you have completed ten lunges on each side and 20 frog jumps.

JUMP SQUATS

A. Stand with your feet slightly wider than a shoulder's distance apart. Squat down while sticking your butt out. Keep your knees just above—not in front of—your toes.

B. Spring up while thrusting your arms overhead. Tap your heels together and then bring your feet apart before you land on your heels, rolling forward onto your toes. Complete 15 repetitions.

REVERSE LUNGE WITH FRONT KICK

A. Stand with your feet a shoulder width apart. Keep your core stable and weight on your heels. Take a large step back with your right foot, planting and then lowering your body until both legs are bent in right angles. (Note: You'll notice that I'm leaning slightly forward in the down portion of the lunge. I find this brings more focus to the glutes and the hips, making it a more effective exercise.)

B. Exhale as you extend your legs. Lift your right foot, bringing your right knee in toward your chest, and then launch a front kick into the stomach of an imaginary opponent standing directly in front of you. Complete 15 lunges with front kicks with the right leg and then repeat on the left side. Then return to the jump squats, and complete one set each of jump squats and reverse lunges with a side kick.

DAVID'S DUMBBELL WRAPAROUND

A. From a seated position on your stability ball, walk your feet forward and slide your torso down the ball until you come into a bench press position with your upper back and head against the ball, knees bent 90 degrees, and feet on the ground. Grasp a dumbbell in each hand with your arms extended toward the ceiling from your chest.

B. Lower your arms behind your head.

C. Once your arms are parallel with the floor with your palms facing up, bring your arms in a semicircle down toward your hips, all the while keeping your arms parallel to the floor.

D. Bend your elbows and squeeze your hands together above your navel, as if you are hugging your arms around a large oak tree with your palms facing each other. Return to the starting position and repeat 20 to 30 times. Remain in the bench press position on the stability ball, and proceed to the next exercise.

David's Inverted Dumbbell Chest Press

A. From your bench press position on the stability ball, bend your elbows out to the sides with a dumbbell in each hand. Your arms should be bent in 90-degree angles. Rotate your hands so your palms are facing in the direction of your head.

B. Press your hands toward the ceiling. As you extend your arms, rotate your hands so your palms are facing your feet. As you lower your arms, rotate your hands back to the starting position. Repeat 20 to 30 times. Remain in the bench press position, and proceed to the next exercise.

Dumbbell Skull Crushers on Ball

A. From your bench press position on the ball, grasp a dumbbell in each hand and bend your right elbow just over your head toward the floor.

B. Keeping your right elbow bent, lower your right hand toward the floor behind your head and rest at about ear level. (Note: Make sure to keep your left arm extended over your chest.)

C. Extend your arm and then bend your elbow again, this time lowering your left hand toward your right nipple. Continue alternating the B and C positions for 20 to 30 repetitions. Then repeat with the other arm. Remain in the bench press position for the next exercise.

INCLINE DUMBBELL PRESS ON BALL

A. From the bench press position, bend your knees and slide your torso down the ball slightly until you come into an incline press position with your knees bent about 90 degrees, your feet on the floor under your knees, and your low and mid back against the ball. Grasp a dumbbell in each hand with your elbows bent and hands by your shoulders.

B. Extend your arms as you slowly press the dumbbells in a straight line directly out from your chest. Lower to the starting position and repeat 20 to 30 times.

BENCH DIPS ON BALL

A. Sit on the floor. Place your heels or calves on top of the stability ball. Place your palms on the floor behind your hips with your fingers facing forward.

B. Press your body weight into your palms as you extend your elbows and lift your buttocks off the floor. Bend your elbows as you lower your buttocks toward the floor without touching. Then extend your elbows and repeat 20 to 30 times. Keep your heels against the ball and proceed to the reverse plank.

REVERSE PLANK

With your heels against the ball and your palms on the floor, press into your hands as you extend your arms and legs, coming into a reverse plank position. Reach up through your hips and sternum. Hold for 15 seconds. Lower and return to the bench dips, completing one to two more sets of the dips and the reverse plank.

DAVID'S ULTIMATE SHOULDER SHAPER I

A. Lie with your chest or tummy against the stability ball (whichever is more comfortable for you). Place the bottoms of your feet against a wall for support. (As you grow stronger, you can do this exercise without the wall, for a greater challenge.) Grasp a dumbbell in each hand, placing your hands just above the floor with your arms extended above your shoulders.

B. Raise the dumbbells until your arms are parallel with the floor and in a straight line from your shoulders.

c Bring your arms around in a semicircle until they are extended from your shoulders at right angles to your torso.

D. Lower the dumbbells to the floor. Then reverse the process, lifting the dumbbells to the right angle position at shoulder height and bringing them around in front. Complete 20 to 30 repetitions.

DAVID'S ULTIMATE SHOULDER SHAPER II

A. Lie with your left side against the stability ball. Scissor your legs to give yourself a wide base for support. Place your left arm around the ball for balance. Grasp a dumbbell in your right hand with your upper arm against your side.

B. Lift the dumbbell toward the ceiling until it is extended from your shoulder. Lower and repeat 20 to 30 times.

HYPEREXTENSIONS

A. Lie with your tummy against the stability ball. Place the bottoms of your feet against a wall for support. (As you grow stronger, you can do this exercise without the wall for a greater challenge.) Hold a dumbbell in each hand, with your elbows bent out to the sides and hands near your ears.

B. Extend your back as you reach your head, shoulders, and elbows toward the ceiling. Lower and repeat 15 to 20 times. Remain in this position for the following exercise.

WIDE DUMBBELL ROWS

A. With your tummy or chest against the ball and feet against the wall, grasp a dumbbell in each hand. Place your hands on the floor below your shoulders.

B. Bend your elbows out to the sides as you raise the dumbbells, as if you are rowing a boat. Lower to the starting position.

C. Lift the dumbbells again, but this time keep your elbows in close to your torso.

Alternate the B and C positions for a total of 15 to 20 repetitions in each position.

Return to the hyperextensions and do one to two more sets of each exercise.

SPIDERMAN PUSH-UPS

A. I feel the need to give credit where credit is due. Ronnie is one of my trainers at the Madison Square Club, and this is one of the exercises I have seen him use with his clients. It is very effective but quite humbling and torturous. Kneel on all fours with your knees under your hips and your hands under your chest. Extend your right arm and left leg.

B. Crawl forward, as Spiderman would crawl up a wall, extending your opposite limbs. Each time you crawl forward, lower yourself into an off-center push-up. For example, if your right arm and left leg are extended, bend both elbows and lower your chest to the floor. Complete 20 total repetitions.

PLYOMETRIC PUSH-UPS

A. Come into a push-up position with your knees and shins against the floor and your palms on the floor under your chest. (As you grow stronger, you can do plyometric push-ups with your legs extended and knees off the floor). Lower yourself into a push-up.

B. With a sudden, explosive burst, push yourself up, lifting your hands off the floor and clapping them together. Complete 10 to 15 repetitions. Complete another set of Ronnie's push-ups followed by another set of plyometric push-ups before proceeding to the next exercise.

FORWARD AND REVERSE CROSSOVER LUNGES WITH BICEPS CURLS

A. Stand with your feet shoulder distance apart. Grasp a dumbbell in each hand. Extend your arms down at your sides.

B. Take a large step diagonally forward with your right foot, planting your foot at the eleven o'clock position. Sink down until your thighs form right angles. As you bend your knees, curl the dumbbells toward your upper arms.

C. Extend your legs, then lift your right knee and bring it in toward your chest as you lower your arms. Step back with your right leg, this time lunging behind your torso and stepping back to the eight o'clock position. As you sink down into the reverse lunge, complete another biceps curl. Repeat 15 to 20 times with the right leg and then switch to lunging with the left leg, stepping forward to the one o'clock position and back to the five o'clock position.

PLIÉ SQUAT WITH CONCENTRATION CURL

A. Stand with your feet slightly wider than hip distance apart. Turn your toes out and your heels in. Grasp a dumbbell in each hand, holding your hands at your hips.

B. Bring your body weight back onto your heels as you bend your knees and squat down while pushing your butt out.

c. Hold the plié squat as you extend your arms laterally from your shoulders. Keeping your upper arms parallel to the floor at all times, curl your hands in toward your shoulders. Complete 20 to 30 biceps curls as you simultaneously squat.

LEG SCISSORS

A. Sit with your legs straight out in front of you, your hands about a foot behind your buttocks, your fingers pointing forward. Lean back slightly, creating a 45-degree angle between your torso and the floor. Bend your knees and bring them in toward your chest so that you can stabilize your core. (Note: If you have lower back problems, you may just want to hold this position and not proceed to the scissors.)

B. Extend your legs until they form a 45-degree angle with the floor.

C. Scissor your legs back and forth, alternating bringing your right leg over your left and left over your right. Move your legs up and down an imaginary ladder, scissoring them as high as you can and as low as you can, and everywhere in between. Continue to scissor your legs for 30 seconds.

SIDE CRUNCH ON BALL

A. Lie with your left side against the stability ball. Scissor your legs so your right leg crosses over your left, giving you a wide base of support. Place your left palm against your abdomen or waist. Grasp a small medicine ball in your right hand. Hold the ball at eye level with your elbow bent.

B. Crunch sideways in a small upward movement as your eyes follow the movement of the medicine ball. Lower and repeat 15 to 20 times and then switch sides.

CONCENTRATED CRUNCH ON BALL WITH MEDICINE BALL

A. Lie with your lower back against the stability ball, your knees bent at 90 degree angles, and your feet flat on the floor. Most of your upper torso should be off the ball, with just your low back and the top edge of your buttocks pressed into the ball. Hold a medicine ball over your chest with both hands. Tuck in your tailbone.

B. Lift your face toward the ceiling as you crunch upward, making sure to keep your tailbone tucked in and buttocks firm. Lower and repeat 15 to 20 times.

DOUBLE CRUNCH WITH BALL

A. Lie with your back on the floor. Hug a stability ball between your knees and shins. Grasp a medicine ball with your arms extended overhead. Bend your knees, and lift your feet off the floor until your thighs are perpendicular to your torso.

B. Exhale as you simultaneously curl your tailbone toward your naval, lift the stability ball toward the ceiling, crunch your upper body upward, and bring the medicine ball toward your knees, as if you were trying to throw the medicine ball at the stability ball (but don't release your grip on the medicine ball). Lower and repeat 10 to 15 times.

After you complete your routine, stretch for at least 3 to 5 minutes, following the cooldown stretching series discussed later in this chapter.

ULTIMATE MAKEOVER ABDOMEN, CORE, AND BACK ROUTINE

Complete the following 15-minute toning routine two days a week, according to the schedule provided in "Your Ultimate Body Calendar," to firm, sculpt, and shrink your abdomen, waist, and low back. I've included some of the most challenging—and most effective—exercises ever invented with all the appropriate tweaks to target the abs. Many of the movements are creations that I've designed for my clients who, over the years, complained that their abs, waist, and love handles were their most pesky pet peeve area.

Persevere with this toning routine, and I guarantee you'll see results. Remember to keep your mind-body connection engaged. It's easy to let your focus wander. Resist that urge and keep your brain in your abs, sides, or back at all times.

GOOD MORNINGS

A. Stand with your feet under your hips. Grasp your stability ball in both hands over your head.

B. With your knees slightly bent, bend forward from the hips, keeping your arms by your ears. Stop once your torso creates a 90-degree angle. Stretch forward through the top of your head and fingertips and back through your tailbone. Keep your back flat and abs tight. Hold 20 to 30 seconds.

GOOD MORNINGS WITH ROTATION

A. Stand with your feet under your hips. Grasp the stability ball in both hands over your head. With your knees slightly bent, bend forward from the hips, keeping your arms by your ears. Stop once your torso creates a 90-degree angle. Stretch forward through the top of your

head and fingertips and back through your tailbone. Keep your back flat and abs tight.

B. Lift your right shoulder blade up toward the ceiling as you lower your left shoulder blade toward the floor, rotating from your hips. Continue to stretch forward through the crown of your head and back through your tailbone. Hold for 15 seconds and then repeat on the other side.

PLANK WITH BALL

Place your palms against the top of the stability ball. Extend your legs and balance on the balls of your feet. Note: the closer together you place your feet, the harder your balancing challenge will be. Firm your abs and flatten your lower back. Stretch forward through the crown of your head and back through your heels. Hold 20 to 30 seconds.

DAVID'S ULTIMATE TORSO CRUNCH

A. Lie with your lower back on the ball, knees bent, and feet on the floor. Grasp a small medicine ball in your right hand. Extend your right arm laterally from your right shoulder. Extend your left arm laterally about 45 degrees away from your left hip bone.

B. Exhale as you lift your right shoulder and hand the ball off to your left hand near your hip.

C. Raise your left arm to shoulder level, and lower your right to hip level. Repeat by handing the ball off to your right hand. Continue handing off the ball from one side to the other as you twist your torso up and down, always following the ball with your gaze, for 20 to 30 repetitions.

DOUBLE OBLIQUE CRUNCH

A. Lie with your back on the floor. Bend your elbows out to the sides and place your fingertips behind the back of your head. Bend your knees and lift your feet until your shins are parallel with the floor.

B. Exhale as you crunch your knees in toward your right shoulder as you simultaneously lift your shoulders. Lower and repeat by bringing your knees in toward your left shoulder. Continue alternating left and right for 20 to 30 complete repetitions.

REVERSE OBLIQUE CRUNCH

A. Lie on your back. Place a stability ball between your knees and shins. Extend your legs toward the ceiling, forming a 90-degree angle with your torso. Bend your elbows out to the sides and place your fingertips behind your head.

B. Exhale as you curl your tailbone toward your navel and rotate your legs, bringing your left foot and knee closer to your torso and right foot and knee farther away. Lower and repeat on the other side, bringing your right foot and knee closer to your torso and left foot and knee farther away. Continue to alternate right and left 20 to 30 times.

HANDOFF

A. Lie on your back. Place a stability ball between your knees and shins. Extend your legs toward the ceiling, forming a 90-degree angle with your torso. Extend your arms overhead.

B. Curl your tailbone toward your navel as you lift the ball up, bringing your arms and shoulders up to meet the ball.

C. Grasp the ball between your hands. Hand off the ball to your hands. Lower your hands and the ball to the floor overhead and your legs to the

floor. Repeat by using your arms to lift the ball and hand it back off to your legs. Continue to switch handing it off from your legs to your hands and hands to your legs a total of 10 to 15 times.

MID BACK
HYPEREXTENSIONS ON BALL

A. Lie with your tummy on the stability ball. Place the bottoms of your feet against a wall for support. (As you grow stronger, you can do this exercise without the wall for a greater challenge.) Hold a medicine ball between your hands with your arms extended overhead.

B. Lift from your mid back and up, keeping your tummy against the ball. Lower and repeat 10 to 15 times. Remain in this position for the rear deltoid laterals.

REAR DELTOID LATERALS WITH MEDICINE BALL

A. With your tummy against the ball, grasp a small medicine ball in your right hand. Hug your left arm around the stability ball for support.

B. Lift your right arm out to the side from your shoulder, keeping your elbow partially bent. (Note: As you are keeping your elbows partially bent, your arms will be making an arcing motion.) Lower and repeat 15 to 20 times. Switch arms and repeat. Remain in this position for the lower back challenge.

LOWER BACK CHALLENGE

A. With your lower tummy on the ball, place your palms on the floor in front of the stability ball. Extend your legs behind you with the balls of your feet against the floor.

B. Exhale as you lift your legs until they are in line with your hips. Flex your feet and stretch (the proper terminology is "reach") back through your heels. Hold ten seconds.

C. Without lowering your legs, spread them to a wide angle, continuing to stretch out through your heels. Hold ten seconds.

D. Without lowering your legs, bring your legs together and turn your heels in and toes out. Hold ten seconds.

ULTIMATE MAKEOVER LEG AND BUTT ROUTINE

Complete the following 15-minute toning routine two to three days a week, according to the schedule provided in "Your Ultimate Body Calendar," to firm, sculpt, and shrink your hips, thighs, and buttocks. I've included my most challenging—and most effective—exercises for this body area. Many of the movements are creations that I've designed for my clients who, over the years, complained that their lower half was their most pesky pet peeve area.

As I mentioned with the abdominal routine, persevere and you'll see results. Remember to keep your mind-body connection engaged. It's easy to let your focus wander. Resist that urge, and keep your brain in your thighs, butt, or hips at all times.

LEG LIFT WITH MEDICINE BALL

A. Lie on your right side with your legs extended. Push your hips forward, and contract your buttocks and abs. Prop up your head with your right hand. Place a medicine ball against your left thigh, using your left hand to hold it in place.

B. Exhale as you raise your left leg, pressing out through your heel as you lift and keeping your foot flexed. Inhale as you lower. Repeat 15 to 20 times and then switch sides.

THE CLAM WITH MEDICINE BALL

A. Lie on your right side. Bend both your hips and legs at 90-degree angles, so that your knees are on the same plane as your hips. Prop your head with your right hand. Place a medicine ball against your left thigh, holding it in place with your left hand.

B. Exhale as you lift your top leg. Focus on lifting with your top knee and feeling the burn in your glutes and hips. Inhale as you lower. Repeat 15 to 20 times and then switch sides.

THE CLAM II WITH MEDICINE BALL

A. Lie on your right side. Bend your knees and bring your thighs in line with your torso. Your knees and calves should form a 90 degree angle behind your torso. Prop your head with your right hand. Place a medicine ball against your left thigh, holding it in place with your left hand.

B. Inhale as you lift your top leg. Exhale as you lower. Repeat 15 to 20 times and then switch sides.

INNER THIGH RAISE

A. Lie on your right side. Bend your left leg so that your left shin and knee are resting on the floor just in front of your extended right leg. Push your hips forward and

contract your abs. Prop your head with your right hand and place your left palm against the floor in front of your tummy.

B. Raise your right leg, pressing through your heel and feeling the burn in your right inner thigh. Lower and repeat 15 to 20 times. Switch sides and repeat.

REVERSE PRONE SCISSORS

A. Lie face down on the floor. Spread your legs as far apart as you can.

B. Press your hips into the floor as you exhale and lift your flexed feet up as you squeeze them together in one fluid motion. Continue to squeeze your heels together at the top of the movement. Inhale as you lower. Repeat 15 to 20 times. Remain in this position and

proceed to the Superman. (Note: Unlike regular scissor movements, with reverse prone scissors the concentration is in lifting and squeezing your heels in an upward motion and together simultaneously.)

SUPERMAN WITH MEDICINE BALL

A. With your tummy against the floor and your legs extended, grasp a medicine ball between your ankles, feet, and calves.

B. Press your hips into the floor as you exhale and lift your flexed feet up, squeezing the ball between your ankles as you lift. Lower and repeat 15 to 20 times. Return to the reverse prone scissors, repeating both the scissors and Superman one to two more times.

DONKEY KICKS

A. Kneel on all fours with your hands under your chest and your knees under your hips. Place a medicine ball in the crease behind your left knee, squeezing your calf and thigh together to hold the ball in place.

B. Bring your left knee in toward your chest.

C. Exhale as you press your left foot toward the ceiling, continuing to hold the ball between your calf and your thigh. Alternate between the B and C positions 15 to 20 times.

D. Pulse your leg upward in a micro movement, reaching your right foot toward the ceiling over and over for about 15 seconds. Relax and repeat with your right leg.

HYDRANTS

A. Kneel on all fours with your hands under your chest and your knees under your hips. Place a medicine ball in the crease behind your left knee, squeezing your calf and thigh together to hold the ball in place.

B. Bend your left leg out to the side until your thigh and calf are parallel with the floor. Lower and repeat 15 to 20 times. On the last repetition, hold for 20 to 30 seconds. Repeat with the right leg.

SISSY SQUATS

A. Stand with your feet under your hips. Place a medicine ball between your knees, squeezing your knees into the ball to hold it in place. Shift your weight onto the balls of your feet and place one hand against a wall, door-knob, chair, or table for balance.

B. Bend your knees as you thrust your hips forward and squat downward, further shifting your weight onto the balls of your feet as you squat.

c. Once your shins are just about parallel to the floor, extend your legs by pressing up through the balls of your feet and lift back to the starting position. Lower your heels and repeat 10 to 15 times. (Note: Although I love sissy squats and think they are a great quadriceps shaper, they are definitely contraindicated if you have any knee problems!)

BRIDGE WITH STABILITY BALL

A. Lie with your back on the floor. Place your heels on top of the stability ball. Rest your hands about 90 degrees away from your sides with your palms facing down.

B. Lift your hips toward the ceiling until only your head, shoulders, and arms are in contact with the floor. Pulse upward through your hips over and over for 20 to 30 seconds. Remain in this position, and proceed to the hamstring curls.

HAMSTRING CURLS

From the bridge position, bend your knees and pull the ball in toward your buttocks. Push the ball back out into the bridge position. Repeat ten times. Remain in this position, and proceed to the one-leg hamstring curls.

ONE-LEG HAMSTRING CURLS

A. From the bridge position, raise your left leg toward the ceiling, balancing on your right heel, shoulders, arms, and head.

B. Bend your right knee and pull the ball in toward your buttocks. Extend your leg as you press the ball away. Repeat five to ten times. Then switch legs and repeat. Remain in this position and proceed to the pelvic tilt.

Pelvic Tilt

A. From the bridge position, bend both knees and bring the ball in toward your buttocks. Place your feet flat on the ball and reach up through your hips as high as you can.

B. Extend your left leg toward the ceiling. Tuck in your tailbone. Hold 15 to 20 seconds. Lower your left foot to the ball and extend your right leg to the ceiling. Hold 15 to 20 seconds.

Butt Squeeze

A. Lie on your back and place a medicine ball between your knees.

B. Squeeze from your buttocks as you exhale, curling your pelvis, tucking in your tailbone, and lifting your hips slightly. Hold for a few seconds and release. Make sure to keep your lower back relaxed as you squeeze the ball. Repeat 10 to 15 times.

STANDING ASYMMETRICAL LUNGES

A. Stand with your feet under your hips. Place a sturdy chair behind you. Reach back with your left leg and place the ball of your left foot on top of the chair. Place your hands on your hips for support.

B. Bend your right knee as you sink into a lunge. Repeat 15 to 20 times and then switch legs.

IRISH JIG

A. Stand with your feet under your hips. Place a medicine ball between your feet.

B. Hop from one side of the medicine ball to the other, placing one foot on top of the ball as you hop from side to side. Do this for 30 seconds.

COOLDOWN
STRETCHING SERIES

Complete the following series of stretches after your cardio sculpting, cardio, and toning routines. You can also do this stretching sequence any time you need to rejuvenate and wake up your body. I like to periodically take a stretch break after working at my desk for a long period of time. Many of my clients tell me they like to do this stretching sequence before bed as well.

CHEST OPENER

Sit with your legs crossed. Place your hands behind your buttocks with your fingers pointing forward. Press down into your palms as you lift up through your sternum. Reach down through your shoulder blades and open your chest. Hold for 20 seconds.

SHOULDER STRETCH

Sit with your legs crossed. Place your right palm along your outer left shoulder. Use your left hand to gently pull your right elbow to the left to increase the stretch. Hold 20 seconds. Repeat with the left arm.

TRICEPS STRETCH

Sit with your legs crossed. Reach your right arm overhead, bringing your right bicep near your right ear. Bend your right elbow and give yourself a pat on the back. With your left hand, pull your right elbow back and over to increase the stretch. Hold 20 seconds and then repeat with the left arm.

GROIN STRETCH

Sit on the floor with the bottoms of your feet pressed together. Allow your knees to drop down. Hold onto the tops of your feet, using your hands to pull your pelvis forward, flattening your back. To increase the stretch, bend forward. Hold 20 seconds.

WIDE ANGLE STRETCH

A. Sit with your legs spread at a wide angle. Make sure your toes and knees point up toward the ceiling. Place your palms on the floor on either side of your torso. Press down into your palms as you lengthen through your spine and rotate the top of your pelvis forward, bringing your tailbone back and up. Try to keep your pelvis in this position as you release your hands.

B. Place one hand to the outside of your right thigh and one to the inside of the thigh. Twist your torso to the right and bend forward over your right leg. Hold 20 seconds.

C. Place one hand to the outside of your left thigh and one to the inside. Twist your torso to the left and bend forward over your left leg. Hold 20 seconds.

D. Bend forward to the middle between your legs as you walk your hands forward, keeping your back long and flat and moving your tailbone back and up. Hold 20 seconds.

BUTTOCKS STRETCH

Sit in modified cross-legged position, placing your right shin directly on top of your left shin, so your legs form a triangle. Flex your right foot. To increase the stretch, bend forward. Hold 20 seconds. Rise and repeat with the left leg on top.

THIGH STRETCH

Lie on one side with your bottom leg extended. Prop your head on your hand for comfort. Bend your top leg behind you, bringing your top foot toward your buttocks, grasping it with your top hand. Hold 20 seconds and repeat on the other side.

ABDOMINAL STRETCH

Kneel with your feet and shins against the floor. Lift your torso until your thighs are perpendicular to the floor. Raise your arms overhead, clasping your hands. Reach up through your palms. Hold 20 seconds.

Well, how do you feel? These should've been the most challenging and exhausting series of exercise routines you have ever completed. Now, you are ready to take on almost any physical and mental challenge. Pat yourself on the back—you did a great job! Don't put down the book so fast! Now that you've completed one of the most grueling exercise programs, let's complement that with the New York Body Plan nutrition section. For the ultimate results, you will need to follow both the training and nutrition components.

4

THE ULTIMATE BODY
NUTRITION PLAN

This morning I met with one of the women on the two-week Ultimate New York Body Plan. Today was the sixth day into her program, and things seem to be progressing rather smoothly—too smoothly in fact! I noticed a somewhat glazed look in her eyes and a slight case of carb face/carb eyes. If you are unfamiliar with those terms, they refer to someone who has indulged in either too many processed carbs or starchy carbs and is paying the price the morning after. I asked, "Did you drink last night?" She sheepishly replied, "Yes, but it wasn't as bad as it could've been."

Her slip was rather simple, but potentially very costly. Instead of the chips and guacamole, she opted for three glasses of white wine. She committed the first of the cardinal sins of nutrition (see "The A, B, C, D, E, and F of Nutrition" later in this chapter). I told her, "You play, you're going to pay."

As you'll soon learn, alcohol consumption is a real no-no on this program. With just two weeks to see results, there is no margin for error. To succeed on this program, you must know your limitations and learn how to work around them. I never use the word *diet*. It's a four-letter word that often leads to temptation, cheating, and failure. Rather, we need to approach our nutrition, the foods and drink we consume, in a more healthful way. Following this plan, you will eat frequent small, healthful meals, and you will metabolize your food (burn your fuel) more efficiently and, consequently, have increased energy. Additionally, by eating smaller, more frequent balanced meals and combining this with my exercise program, you will be raising your metabolism, stoking your machine (body), burning more calories, and reducing your body fat.

Although I don't refer to my program as a diet, you must follow my A, B, C, D, E, and F of nutrition. Don't get me wrong. You will not be starving yourself, and, in fact, you may choose from two different nutrition plans. The first option is more stringent and therefore more challenging. It involves consuming two relatively low-carb meal replacement shakes, two snacks, and one protein and vegetable meal a day. If you are not a shake person, then I have included real food options that may be used in place of the shakes. The two plans are similar in their caloric content and their overall effect on the body.

I must caution you that this program is extreme. I don't want you doing this if you're not ready. Food is essential for life, but, as with many things in life, too much of a good thing is not always good. I live by two mantras when dealing with nutrition: (1) "If some is good, more is not necessarily better"; and (2) "Less is more, and more is often too much!" By fully embracing the meaning of both these mantras, you will have a much easier time successfully following this two-week nutrition plan. Not only are you now transforming your physical body with the most intense, challenging workouts, but you are enriching it with the most delicious and nutritious foods. You will be empowered with the knowledge and confidence to carry out and maintain your amazing results beyond the two weeks and into the rest of your life.

HOW THE NUTRITION PLAN WORKS

Your nutrition plan works synergistically with your fitness plan to help you achieve ultimate results. Just as your fitness plan will work you to your edge—and beyond—your nutrition plan is equally challenging. There are lots of diets out there that promise to allow you to eat all the foods you love and still lose weight. Well, you know what? They don't work. Sure, such diets might help someone who is extremely overweight to lose a few pounds, but will they help you trim off the last five pounds in order to fit into a wedding dress or bikini or to look stunning at a high school reunion? And those diets will not give you lasting results. Stop the diet yo-yoing. Forget those fad diets!. I'll be honest with you. To get ultimate results, you're going to have to make some sacrifices. That means giving up some of your favorite foods for the next two weeks. It's that simple. For me, it meant no biscotti, not even one was allowed. It felt like an onerous punishment, but by the end of the two weeks, the end had definitely justified the means. Again, Mom's words come ringing through loud and clear, "Anything worth having is worth working for."

I based this eating plan on the latest science of the physiology of fat burning and appetite. At the heart of the plan is an extremely low-carbohydrate diet. Although nutritionists and many experts have pooh-poohed low-carbohydrate diets for many years, a wealth of research published during the past two years has countered just about any claim ever made against low-carb diets. The naysayers had claimed that low-carb diets would result in kidney problems. Not so. The naysayers said low-carb diets would raise the risk for heart disease. Not so.

Perhaps most convincing is the growing number of studies that show low-carbohydrate diets are the most efficient and most satisfying way to lose weight and keep it off. In addition to eating very few carbohydrates during the next two weeks, you'll also be eating extremely cleanly. In other words, all the food you put in your mouth will be as fresh as possible, and as low in fat as possible, and it will contain as little processing as possible. For the next two weeks, you'll eat a diet rich in lean protein and low-calorie and fiber-rich vegetables. You'll have small amounts of healthful fats every day. You won't, however, be eating cakes, cookies, desserts, fried chicken, bacon, butter, fruit, cheese, milk, sweet potatoes, or bread. I'll soon explain why all those foods hinder your progress. First, however, let's take a look at the latest science of fat burning, metabolism, and appetite control.

PROTEIN MAKES A COMEBACK

Countless clinical trials by the most accredited researchers and universities in the country have concluded that, lo and behold, low carb is the real deal.

Though most had sought to discredit the low carb phenomenon, all have since realized that restricting carbohydrate intake is no mere fad diet, but rather is a true scientific advancement for the new millennium.

During the 1990s, high-carbohydrate, low-fat diets were all the rage. At the time, scientists blamed the high amounts of saturated fats in the American diet for our bulging waistlines and skyrocketing rates of heart disease. A plethora of low-fat and nonfat products soon hit the supermarket shelves, from nonfat cookies to baked potato chips. The U.S. government led the charge by releasing its Food Guide Pyramid in 1992, a nutrition plan that placed grains and other carbs at the base. Americans caught on quickly to the new trend and cut back on meat, switched from whole milk to skim, and gave up their chocolate chip cookies for reduced fat cookies.

As more and more people turned to pasta, rice, bagels, and nonfat snacks, more and more people got fat. I'll never forget the first model I ever worked with. She came in one day and proudly announced that she had eaten really well the night before: just one box of nonfat crackers, a one-pound container of nonfat cottage cheese, and a box of reduced-fat cookies. In her mind, she had eaten really well because she had consumed almost no grams of fat. This is just one classic example of how Americans were really duped in the 1980s and the 1990s into believing that fat was the only culprit making us fat. Although some people certainly were able to lose weight during these low-fat years, the vast majority of Americans porked out. Perplexed, scientists went back to the drawing board, trying to figure out where things went wrong. After many years of research, scientists have made some interesting discoveries. Those discoveries include the following.

LOW FAT DOESN'T EQUAL LOW CALORIE   One of the reasons nutrition scientists began promoting low-fat, high-carbohydrate diets was that each gram of fat contains 9 calories, compared to carbohydrate's 4. They reasoned that simply switching from high-fat foods to high-carbohydrate foods would automatically lower the overall caloric intake, thus resulting in weight loss. Well, this didn't happen for a number of reasons.

First, thanks to the addition of sugar and high fructose corn syrup, many low-fat, high-carbohydrate foods are not lower in calories than their high-fat counterparts. For instance, to make low-fat cookies taste good, manufacturers added more sugar in place of the fat. From a calorie standpoint, low-fat cookies are just as bad for your waistline as high-fat cookies. Second, most people eat a larger portion size of low-fat foods than they do of high-fat foods, possibly under the false belief that low fat equals low calorie. Think about it. If you were scooping some low-fat ice cream into a bowl, would you scoop out the same amount as you would high-fat ice cream? Probably not. You'd reward yourself for eating the low-fat ice cream by adding an extra scoop, which brings me to my third point. High-carb, low-fat foods are not as satisfying as their original counterparts. In the end, many people consume more calories on a low-fat diet than when on a high fat diet. Because it is often the fat that makes certain foods more satiating, I've included foods such as raw almonds in this nutrition program.

NOT ALL FATS ARE BAD Not only was cutting fat out of the diet not the answer, but it was shortsighted. There are many different types of fat, ranging from the artery-clogging saturated fats found in fatty cuts of meat and whole milk to the processed trans fats found in commercially baked goods and margarine (which, by the way, may be worse for your health than butter)—and often in movie popcorn—to the heart-friendly unsaturated fats found in certain vegetables, nuts, flaxseed, and fish. As it turns out, unsaturated fats may also promote weight loss. When researchers compared diets rich in maize (corn) oil, beef tallow, and fish oil, they found that rats who ate the diet rich in fish oil gained less weight than rats on the beef or corn oil diet. Other studies show that replacing saturated and trans fats with unsaturated fats results in weight loss, even when total caloric intake is held constant. Unsaturated fats are also better for your heart. Eating unsaturated fats instead of saturated or trans fats lowers your unhealthy LDL cholesterol and lowers levels of triglycerides (a nasty type of blood fat).

NOT ALL CALORIES ARE EQUAL Now, here's where the really amazing discoveries took place. For many years, scientists told us that to lose weight, you had to eat fewer calories than you burned. Well that's true to a point. Some of the calories you eat are more likely to lead to weight gain than others. For instance, certain foods use more energy during the process of digestion than others. Any time you eat, your body must burn calories in order to break the food down, push it through your intestines, and absorb its nutrients. Researchers now know that your body burns roughly 40 more calories per meal if your meal is high in protein compared to one that's high in carbohydrate or fat. Researchers also know that high-protein foods tend to cause a slow, even rise in blood sugar, whereas carbohydrates cause blood sugar levels to spike. The slower your blood sugar rises, the less of the hormone insulin your pancreas must secrete to clear the sugar out of your blood. Among other things, insulin triggers fat storage and hunger. This is why you feel hungry not long after eating a bagel, even though that bagel contains roughly 400 calories. On the other hand, try eating 400 calories of egg whites (that's about 14 egg whites!). You won't feel hungry again for hours.

Highly processed carbohydrates—the type you find in boxes, shrink-wrap, and other packaging in the middle aisles of the grocery store—are about the worst thing you can eat when it comes to losing weight and looking your best. These carbs are all made from white flour and white sugar, both of which are highly processed. To create white flour, the processor starts with wheat, an otherwise healthy food. However, once you remove the hull and outer covering, you're left with just the inside of the grain, which contains no fiber and few, if any, nutrients. It's no better for you than table sugar. The lack of fiber and high number of calories in processed carbohydrates cause them to hit your bloodstream faster than just about any other food you can eat.

Researchers have tested hundreds of foods and ranked them for their speed in spiking blood sugar levels on a scale known as the *glycemic index*. Foods that rank high on the index, such as table sugar and potatoes, spike blood sugar quickly. Foods that rank low on the index, such as beans and most vegetables, cause a slow, even rise in blood sugar. On my Ultimate New York Body Plan, you will eat only low-glycemic carbs for two weeks. After two weeks, you will focus most of your diet on low-glycemic carbs, reserving high-glycemic carbs for special occasions and treats.

So now you can see why this nutrition plan is rich in protein and very low in carbohydrates. The protein in this diet will help you in a number of ways:

■ PRESERVING AND BUILDING MUSCLE MASS Usually when you cut back on calories, your body responds by cannibalizing muscle tissue and sparing fat tissue. This is destructive because your muscle tissue runs your metabolism. Each pound of muscle you lose results in 35 to 50 fewer calories a day that your body burns for energy. Numerous studies, however, show that increasing the amount of protein in your diet helps preserve muscle mass, even when calorie intake is very, very low.

■ PREVENTING HUNGER Protein takes longer to digest than do carbohydrates, so it will help you feel satisfied for a longer period of time, preventing cravings and overeating. In one study, researchers split formerly obese participants who had recently lost a considerable amount of weight into two groups, with one group eating 48 more grams of protein a day than the other. Both groups consumed the same number of total calories. After four weeks, those in the high-protein group regained half as much weight as the higher-carb group and reported increased satisfaction after their meals.

■ BOOSTING YOUR METABOLISM As I mention earlier, your body burns more calories to digest protein than it does to digest carbohydrates or fat.

Mind you, this is not like other high-protein diets that tell you to eat absolutely no carbs but to eat any type of protein you want. You will eat some carbs, but they will all be low in sugar and calories and high in fiber (such as broccoli and spinach). Conversely, the protein you eat will be lean and very low in saturated fat. Let's take a look more specifically at what you will not be eating during the next two weeks and why.

THE A, B, C, D, E, AND F OF NUTRITION

Usually, my rule of thumb is the phrase, "Never say never." By that, I mean that you don't need to ban any particular food from your diet. You just need to eat some foods rarely, and then sparingly. As with the exercise plan, however, every rule has an exception. For the next two weeks, you will say "never" to many foods. When you are looking for extreme results, you must make extreme sacrifices. In order to get the results you seek, you must strictly adhere to the following A, B, C, D, E, and F of nutrition.

A. Alcohol. You may have read that alcohol is good for your heart and that it reduces blood cholesterol levels. That doesn't make it good for your waistline. A standard mixed drink contains 100 to 250 calories. That's only the half of it. Most people eat more when they drink. So while you may think that you can compensate for your glass of wine by eating less for dinner, it rarely works out that way. Often alcohol makes you crave the very foods you are trying to avoid. Why drink something that will erode your willpower?

Your body also processes alcohol differently from the way it does other carbs. That's right, alcohol is a carb. Made from fermented wheat, barley, grapes, or some other carbohydrate ingredient, alcohol contains more sugar than most people bargain for. Yet, your body treats alcohol differently from the way it treats sugar. First of all, alcohol contains 7 calories per gram, compared to 4 calories per gram in most carbs. Your body treats alcohol as a toxin, so your liver processes alcohol calories before all others in an attempt to clean the toxins from your bloodstream. As other calories wait on line, your body senses a rise in calories and shuttles many of them into your fat cells, which is exactly what you don't want.

Alcohol is the absolute worst drink you can have when you are putting your body in a carb-deprived state. It will make you crave carbs. Think about the foods you tend to eat not only while you are drinking, but also the day after drinking. Alcohol almost always starts off a carb binge. For all these reasons and more, alcohol is on the "do not eat or drink" list. Stay off it for two weeks. There are no exceptions. No wine, no beer, no coolers. No cheating. In the maintenance chapter, you'll learn how to bring alcohol back onto your menu, but I'll tell you right now, you'll want to minimize your drinking for the rest of your life in order to maintain your results. You might as well get used to that idea right now.

If you generally need alcohol to unwind or blow off steam, find another outlet for your emotions—such as a hard cardio sculpting workout. Before you put the book down and start heading for the door, relax and sit tight. I realize that this all-or-nothing approach to alcohol may not be very realistic. Even my mother likes a little glass of champagne (rosé preferably) every now and again. I'll make a deal with you. You give me two weeks of no alcohol, and I'll give you some tips in the maintenance chapter on how to drink more healthfully.

B. Bread. The last time you ate at an Italian restaurant, were you able to hold yourself to just one piece of bread from the bread basket? Few people ever do. Bread is one of the biggest binge starters around. It's filled with empty carbs that spike your blood sugar, sending your body into fat storage mode and increasing your sensations of hunger. In short, bread is empty, wasted calories. Most types of bread really pack on the calories. For example, most bagels contain more than 400 calories. Just one slice of white bread contains 100 calories. I am also throwing crackers (regular and fat free) in the forbidden Bs. They deceptively pack a mean punch of carbohydrates and often sodium and, usually, trans fats. On the maintenance plan in Chapter 7, you'll learn how to bring certain types of bread back into your life.

C. Starchy Carbs. Carrots, potatoes, rice, pasta, and corn all contain high amounts of carbohydrates and rank high or relatively high on the glycemic index. For the next two weeks, you'll be cutting all starchy carbs out of your diet, including high-fiber, whole grain carbs such as brown rice and quinoa. In the maintenance program in Chapter 7, you'll learn which starchy carbs are safe to reintroduce to your diet and which ones are not.

Being of eastern European descent (that's meat and potato country), this restriction is often the hardest for me to adhere to. Not a solitary meal that Grandma prepared was devoid of starchy carbohydrates in the form of kugel, pancakes, or mashed potatoes. I will tell you this with complete certainty: Eating a meal without the starches will leave you feeling sated but light, alert, and without the typical tummy bloating that those starches often bring. Of course, it took my entire freshman year of college for me to attribute the pains in my stomach to excessive carbohydrate consumption. Once realized, it was smooth sailing and a two-size reduction in my jeans.

D. Dairy. Many people don't realize that dairy products contain high amounts of a sugar called lactose. Not only that, but most people are sensitive to this sugar and can't digest it well. It leads to bloating, which is the last thing you want when you want to look your best. On the other hand, dairy products are high in the mineral calcium, which is an important component of fat burning. To make sure you consume enough calcium in your diet over the next two weeks, you'll take a calcium supplement and consume nondairy sources of calcium such as broccoli, almonds, and sardines. (I love fresh sardines. When you're in New York City, you'll have to try the fresh grilled sardines at Da Silvano. Silvano's has the most artful touch with fresh sardines!)

E. Extra Sweets. Any sweet food can lead to carbohydrate cravings, including sugar substitutes. On the Ultimate New York Body Plan, you will avoid all sources of sugar, high fructose corn syrup, and sugar substitutes. That means no fruit juice, no diet or regular soda, no artificial sweeteners, no honey, and no molasses. If you crave a sweet taste, then try an herbal tea such as one with peppermint or vanilla flavor.

WHY I DON'T BELIEVE IN SUGAR SUBSTITUTES

Some diets encourage you to use sugar substitutes and drink diet soda. I don't. For one, I don't believe in fake food. If the ingredient label contains a list of words I can't pronounce or define, I don't eat that food. This is especially true with sugar substitutes such as sorbitol, saccharin, and aspartame. Eating fake sugar will forever keep you dependent on the taste of sweetness. You'll never be able to wean yourself off your carb cravings. Worse, some research indicates that sugar substitutes create the same surge in insulin, the fat storage hormone, as the real thing.

F. Fruit and Most Fats. A recent client of mine couldn't understand why she was putting on weight. It become abundantly clear to me as we spoke that she was consuming too much fruit. Remember, if some is good, more is not necessarily better. You might be thinking, "Fruit is good for me. It's good for my heart. Why cut out fruit?" Fruit, my friend, contains high amounts of fructose, a sugar, and more calories than you need when you are trying to sculpt the best body of your life. In the maintenance chapter (Chapter 7), you will learn which fruits can be reintroduced into your diet.

As for fat, you'll be nearly eliminating the artery-clogging saturated and trans fats and focusing exclusively on certain types of unsaturated fats. You'll eat no red meat, pork, bacon, or other types of fatty meats. Instead, all your protein will be lean: skinless chicken breast, egg whites, fresh roasted turkey breast, turkey bacon, wild salmon, fresh tuna, halibut, and striped bass, to name a few. You'll eat no processed foods, including any of the plethora of low-carb products that are now stacked on your supermarket shelves. These foods are not regulated by the FDA, and many of them contain more carbs than you bargain for. Nuts are good and satisfying, and the Ultimate Body Plan prescribes 7 to 10 raw almonds a day. Not only will you be getting a great supply of fiber (which will help keep you regular), but almonds have a higher concentration of vitamin E than any other food. You can also use up to a teaspoon of olive oil a day, as a dressing for your salad. For these two weeks, you will stay away from additional unsaturated fats such as avocados, olives, peanut butter, and egg yolks. Although all these foods are healthy, they all contain high amounts of calories.

In addition to staying away from the banned foods I have named, you also will be making your own meals for the next two weeks. That means brown-bagging it to work, cooking dinner, and making breakfast. Cooking your own food is the surest way to guarantee that your food complies with your nutrition plan. That's not to say that if you aren't able to prepare your own meals, the program will not work for you. The best-case scenario is, of course, doing it yourself. If you must eat out, be mindful of how and why you are eating, and you will be able to eat out intelligently and safely.

Finally, I recommend you give up any flavored beverage, including diet soda, and switch to water. Water has no calories and can be quite filling.

Make sure to drink one or two glasses before each meal. Add a squeeze of lemon or lime for flavor. Or try an herbal tea.

One final note—and I know you're not going to be happy—with respect to coffee. As much as I know that you love that morning jolt, it may be doing some not so beneficial things to your body. The caffeine in coffee raises the cortisol levels in your blood, causing your insulin to rise and your blood sugar to spike. This is not a good thing and may actually cause you to store body fat. Switching to green tea may just be the answer. Green tea contains enough caffeine to wake you up, but not so much that it spikes cortisol levels. It also delivers a healthy dose of anticarcinogenic polyphenols, which, science shows, boost metabolism.

A TYPICAL DAY OF ULTIMATE EATING

So now you know what you are *not* going to eat during the next few weeks. What can you put on your breakfast, lunch, and dinner plate? On the Ultimate New York Body Plan, you will eat every three hours, ideally at 7 A.M., 10 A.M., 1 P.M., 4 P.M., and 7 P.M. This will prevent you from getting too hungry, thus preventing cravings and bingeing, and will keep your metabolic furnace burning. It also will keep you motivated and energetic for your workouts.

Let's take a closer look.

Breakfast. You will start off your day with a dose of protein. I recommend you start the day with a protein shake. (See the section "Your Protein Shakes" later in this chapter.) If you're the type of person who does not like to drink your food, then you will start the day with egg whites in the form of an omelet or a frittata. (See the recipes for Scrambled Egg Whites with Shiitake Mushrooms and Turkey Bacon, Scrambled Egg Whites with Ground Turkey and Chopped Tomatoes, Spinach and Broccoli Egg White Frittata, and more in Chapter 6.) Either way, you are putting protein into your system first thing in the morning. This will help you to stick with the Ultimate New

York Body Plan for the rest of the day. In a study of 37 obese children, those who ate low-glycemic foods for breakfast—such as high protein meals—consumed fewer calories during the rest of the day, compared to children who ate high-glycemic foods for breakfast. I wouldn't start my day without an energizing protein shake. I have my first shake of the day at 5 A.M.

I encourage you to give protein a try. Although you may be used to starting the day with carbs, possibly in the form of a doughnut or, maybe slightly better, in the form of cold breakfast cereal, the sounder choice is nutritious protein. It will help you stay satisfied longer. Whereas you probably feel hungry an hour or so after eating a breakfast high in carbohydrate, this high-protein breakfast will keep you satisfied for most of the morning. It will also turn up your metabolic rate because your body burns more calories to digest protein than it does to digest carbohydrates.

If you tend to skip breakfast, you must break yourself of that habit. To keep your metabolism humming along, your body needs regular doses of calories, about every three hours. After sleeping for eight hours, you need to get your metabolism moving, and the only way to do that is to eat. When you deny your body the breakfast that it needs, you start the day with a slower than normal metabolism. Your body senses that a famine is approaching, and it turns down your metabolic rate in order to conserve calories and fat. Also, skipping breakfast allows your blood sugar to plummet, which increases hunger and cravings throughout the day. Nutritionists have long known that people who tend to binge at night, eating the majority of their calories after 7 P.M., are notorious breakfast skippers. If you want to sabotage your success on this program, then go ahead and skip breakfast. It's the surest way to guarantee that you will cheat on the plan later in the day. No matter how frenzied you are in the morning, you can fit in a shake. Drink it during your commute. It's the easiest option around.

Midmorning Snack. To keep your metabolism on the go, you must feed it fuel about every three hours. For staying power, make this snack high in protein, such as 3 ounces of canned tuna (packed in water) or a serving of my low-fat egg salad. Ingesting protein will keep your metabolic rate up and prevent you from feeling the crash (or low) of carb.

Lunch. I'd like you to eat your largest meal of the day at around noon. It's more intelligent to eat as the Italians do, making lunch the biggest meal of the day and giving yourself the rest of the day to work off those calories. Lunch might consist of a lean source of protein, such as 6 ounces of chicken breast or fish, along with half a plate to a full plate of your favorite vegetable such as steamed broccoli or spinach. Or you might create a large salad. Fill a plate with salad greens. Anything goes to make up this salad as long as you stay away from carrots (because of their high carbohydrate content). Add a source of protein to your salad, such as a piece of salmon or tuna, sliced, skinless, grilled chicken breast, or sliced hard-boiled egg whites. Add some vinegar (any variety except balsamic, which contains sugar) along with a teaspoon of olive oil.

Midafternoon Snack. Again, make your midafternoon snack high in protein. You might have 3 ounces of roasted chicken. I love to have seven raw almonds in the afternoon. In one study, subjects on a low-calorie diet supplemented with almonds lost more weight than those on a similar diet without almonds. Avoid almonds, however, if you are one of those people who would have difficulty limiting yourself to just seven.

Dinner. I generally recommend that you end your day with a protein shake, although this depends somewhat on what time you work out (see "Timing Your Meals with Your Workouts" later in this chapter). Ending the day with the shake gives your muscles the amino acids they need to repair themselves while you sleep. It also ensures that you eat the majority of your calories earlier in the day. This way, you won't be digesting food while you sleep, which will help you to sleep better. With all the exercising you are going to be doing for the next two weeks, your sleep quality is extremely important. It's during sleep that the body secretes growth hormone and repairs not only your muscles but also your immune system and other critical systems. Quality sleep will help you to wake refreshed and ready for your next day's exercise session. If you don't want a shake, the meal plan in Chapter 5 includes other food options.

After 7 P.M., put a mental lock on the kitchen and stay away from the fridge. Relax, it's just 14 days—it'll be worth it.

YOUR PROTEIN SHAKES

On the Ultimate New York Body Plan, I recommend you consume two protein shakes a day, partly for convenience. I've noticed time and time again that most people get tripped up not by their exercise plan but by their eating plan. In order to find time to fit in the one to one and a half hours a day of exercise, you are going to need to take time away from something else in your day. For many people it's simply not realistic to try to cook three complete meals and two snacks a day. There just isn't time.

That's the beauty of making two of your meals shakes. It takes just a minute or two to mix up a protein shake. You can drink it wherever you find yourself, during your morning commute or even during a board meeting. I've found that protein shakes have helped my clients wean themselves off the fast-food lifestyle.

Your shake ideally will provide you with the perfect mix of protein, carbs, healthful fats, fiber, and vitamins. When used properly, these powdered meal replacement drinks offer a viable, time-saving meal choice. They will prevent hunger, give you the energy you need for your workouts, keep you satisfied, and provide the amino acids your muscles need to recuperate after your exercise sessions.

The right shake powder will properly reinforce your body and set you on your way. The wrong one, on the other hand, can set you back many calories in the form of carbs, sugar, and fat. There is a major flaw in the critical absence of quality proteins, fats, fiber, and other vital micronutrients in some of today's products associated with low-carb diets. This evaluation of the top sellers in today's market will shed light on the most important aspects of meal replacement drinks, what to look for and what to look out for, what you have been taking and what you have been missing. When studying the ingredient labels of protein drinks, look for the following.

Type of Protein. Protein powders come from many sources, ranging from whey to eggs to bovine colostrums to casein to soy. Whey protein is essentially milk protein without the casein and sugar. I prefer it to other types because your body absorbs it most efficiently. Of all the protein sources, your body digests it most rapidly, shuttling amino acids to your muscles most quickly. In short, this type of protein will help speed your exercise recovery, allow you to sculpt muscle faster, and reduce soreness after your sessions. Of all the protein sources available today, the scientific community and athletes agree that whey protein is best for overall performance.

Cross-flow microfiltered whey protein isolate, with its average yield of 90 percent protein and its near absence of lactose and fat, tops the list, with high-quality *cross-flow microfiltered whey protein concentrate,* with a yield of about 80 percent protein, running a close second. Cross-flow microfiltration is a process by which the proteins are physically separated by microscopic filters, thus avoiding the destruction of the proteins, which is typically what happens with heat or acid separation methods. These high-quality whey proteins contain the highest concentration of intact protein microfractions, including immunoglobins, which help support the body's immune system, placing them at the top of the list for immunoenhancing potential.

THE INSIDE STORY ON WHEY

If whey protein is so good for you, why do so many meal replacement beverages contain "proprietary protein blends"? Whey protein isolate is considerably more expensive than almost all other reliable protein sources except egg albumin, which is considerably lower in bioavailability. For this reason, whey protein isolates are either excluded from the mix or blended with the cheaper, more poorly absorbed "garbage" proteins such as caseinates and milk protein isolates and concentrates. These far lesser quality proteins are also used for their taste appeal. If whey proteins appear in a blend of, let's say, two or three other protein sources, you are more than likely getting a mere spritz of the good stuff in addition to a whole lot of the inferior ingredient.

Whey proteins contain the highest concentration of branched chain amino acids (BCAAs). These amino acids are an integral part of muscle metabolism and are the first aminos sacrificed during muscle catabolism (muscle wasting), a process all too common in most weight loss regimens. Whey protein also enhances glutathione production. Glutathione is the body's most powerful, naturally occurring antioxidant and also plays a role in immune system support.

Carbohydrates. Many of the meal replacement drinks on the market do not seem to focus much attention on the carbohydrate component. Most use high amounts of maltodextrin, a cheap complex carbohydrate derived from corn that burns more like a sugar than a true complex carbohydrate. Some companies even add simple sugars on top of this, such as corn syrup. Needless to say, because of their higher carbohydrate content, such products are incompatible with an effective low-carb diet.

AVOID THE CARB TRAPS

Sugar and carbs hide in a variety of foods you may not suspect. Here are a few of the surprising carb traps:

- BBQ sauce

- Ketchup

- Balsamic vinegar

- Most commercially prepared salad dressings

- Any food that lists high-fructose corn syrup as an ingredient

Flaxseed Oil. Flax contains essential fatty acids, important fats that our bodies can't make on their own and that must be obtained through our diet. These fats are extremely important in literally hundreds of biological processes. Flaxseeds are rich in alpha linolenic acid (an omega-3 essential fatty acid) and linoleic acid (an omega-6 essential fatty acid). These important fats may do the following:

- Increase metabolic rate and fat burning

- Stimulate prostaglandin production (Prostaglandins are hormonelike chemicals produced by the body that exhibit a wide range of critical actions on things like blood pressure, water balance, inflammation, and immune system reactions.)

- Prevent body fat storage

- Increase muscle tone and reduce muscle wasting by encouraging muscle receptors to increase insulin sensitivity

- Significantly increase energy levels and performance through increased blood flow and cardiovascular function

- Decrease water retention

- Help alleviate mood swings and mild depression during dieting

- Increase the absorption of calcium, in part by enhancing the effects of vitamin D

Flax is a dynamite energy source that is high in soluble and insoluble fiber, which helps maintain regularity and healthy cholesterol levels. Flax also contains the highest concentration of lignans of any commercially available material. Lignans are powerful phytonutrients (plant compounds) that support a healthy immune system.

Medium Chain Triglycerides. Other than the essential fatty acids, the only other fat source known for its usefulness in sports is MCTs, or medium chain triglycerides. These medium-length fatty acids are quickly converted to energy. MCTs are highly beneficial for endurance athletes or those on a ketogenic (low-carbohydrate) diet.

Fiber. One of the downsides of a high-protein diet is that it tends to result in constipation. I've included many vegetables in your meal plan to help counteract that tendency. Getting a drink that contains a lot of fiber, and flaxseed in particular, will help keep you regular.

Water Base. Ideally, your shake should come in the form of a protein powder that can be mixed with water. Stay away from shakes that recommend mixing with a juice, such as orange juice, or with yogurt. Both juice and yogurt are on your banned food list.

It's hard to find a commercially available meal replacement powder that meets all the above requirements. I have included a resource section in the back of this book that may help you identify and locate products.

FOR THOSE WHO PREFER TO CHEW

I know that you may not want to drink your calories. You may feel satisfied only after chewing, or perhaps you love to cook. It's OK to eat real food instead of the shakes—as long as you don't turn to fast food! Although the menus in Chapter 6 suggest two shakes a day, you may continue to eat real food with the following substitutions. Here are some options:

- ■ BREAKFAST Your best option for breakfast is egg whites. This will give your body quality protein and all the essential amino acids it needs. I ask you to use egg whites instead of whole eggs because most of the fat and calories of the egg are housed in the yolk. Start off your day with an egg white omelet full of your favorite vegetables. You'll find my favorite egg white omelet and frittata recipes in Chapter 6.

- ■ LUNCH Combine a source of lean protein (6 ounces of salmon, tuna, or chicken breast) with a hearty serving of your favorite steamed vegetable.

- **DINNER** Instead of a shake, you can make yourself a large salad with a lean source of protein. Pile on the vegetables (except for carrots), and place your favorite lean protein on top; this may range from grilled chicken breast to salmon to tuna. You'll find meal suggestions for dinner in Chapter 5.

TIMING YOUR MEALS
WITH YOUR WORKOUTS

Exactly when you have your meals and snacks and shakes depends in part on what time of day you work out. I highly recommend you do your workouts in the morning, and the meal plan in Chapter 5 makes that assumption. Working out in the morning starts you off on the right foot. Research shows that people who exercise in the morning tend to eat better all day long. It sets a mental note that you've already worked hard, why ruin the hard work by eating a brownie? An early morning exercise session also puts your body in fat-burning mode early in the day. I've also found that my early morning clients tend to cancel their sessions less frequently than those who train with me later in the day.

That said, if you need to exercise at a different time of day in order to fit exercise into your schedule, by all means do. Here's how to alter your eating and the menus in Chapter 5 depending on the time of day you work out.

- **THE MORNING WORKOUT** The optimal time to work out on this program is at 7 A.M. because you'll be working out on an empty stomach and burning maximum fat. Drink your protein shake immediately afterward. I am not thrilled with eating before the early morning workout, since I don't think you give yourself time to digest or enough energy for your workout. I'd rather have you have some green tea if energy is what you're searching for. Then you'll have your snack at around 10 A.M.

- **THE MIDAFTERNOON WORKOUT** You want some food in your tank to power your workout, but not so much food that you feel sick and sluggish.

If 4 P.M. is your usual workout time, then I strongly suggest you make lunch your largest meal of the day. This will give you the fuel you need for your workout, preventing the all-too-common excuse of "I'm too hungry to exercise." After your session, drink a protein shake or have your seven almonds or no-fat Dijon egg salad. Then follow up with a small dinner at around 7 P.M.

■ THE EVENING WORKOUT If you exercise at night, your shake will be your last meal. Make sure to have a substantial lunch and protein rich midafternoon snack (such as 4 ounces of chicken or tuna). Follow up with a shake, even if it's after 7 P.M. A protein shake is one of the safest late-night calorie options and will give your muscles what they need to fully recover after your workout.

A FEW EXTRA NUTRIENTS

You'll be cutting back on a lot of wholesome foods for the next two weeks. To make up for the loss of those foods in your diet and to provide the energy you'll need for your workouts, I recommend you supplement your diet with the following on a daily basis.

Antioxidants (Vitamins C and E and Coenzyme Q_{10}) These powerful antioxidants lend their electrons to free radicals in your body, making the radicals more stable and preventing them from destroying cells. This can prevent a host of problems from general aging to heart disease to cancer to arthritis. Your best defense against free radicals is a multilevel approach, and that's why I suggest all the above antioxidants rather than just one. You can get all these antioxidants, plus a dose of other helpful vitamins and minerals, from a few commercially available multivitamin and mineral supplements sold in health food stores. See Chapter 8, Resources.

Ginseng. One of the best energy boosters around, ginseng can also help boost your immunity and overall wellness. Follow package directions.

Vitamin B$_{12}$. You need vitamin B$_{12}$ for energy production. Take a vitamin supplement that provides 100 percent of the daily recommended allowance.

Calcium. For the first two weeks of this program you will be cutting dairy products out of your diet, which is one reason why I suggest you supplement with calcium. A growing amount of research shows that this mineral may be integral to the process of fat-burning. Take a supplement that contains about 500 milligrams of calcium twice a day, because your body can absorb only that much at once. This will give you the amount you need to maintain strong bones as well as boost your fat-burning furnace. You can consume additional calcium in dark green vegetables such as broccoli and spinach.

You'll find a number of weight loss, fat-burning, and energy supplements out there from which to choose. Stay away from supplements with a high caffeine content and other stimulants, such as theobromine. Note that many weight loss supplements contain hidden caffeine in the form of yerba maté, guarana, and green coffee bean extract, totaling the amount of caffeine in five to six cups of coffee!

Also know that many vitamin and mineral supplements contain the sweetener fructose, a very sweet sugar that can spike blood sugar quickly, leading to cravings, hunger, and low energy. Some also contain questionable metals such as nickel and tin. So be sure and read the labels of any supplements that you take while on this program. Again, you can check out Chapter 8 for additional information.

5
THE ULTIMATE BODY
14-DAY PLAN

Welcome to the Ultimate New York Body Plan, and congratulations on making the commitment to life transformation. Throughout each day during the next 14 days, you will be testing your mental, physical, and spiritual strength as you grow and transform into the new you. No matter how hard the program gets, always remember why you embarked on this challenge in the first place. You are worth it, and you have what it takes to persevere. I believe in you.

For each of the next 14 days, I've provided you with some tools to help you stay on track. Each day you will find:

■ AN INSPIRATIONAL PEP TALK These will keep you motivated.

■ YOUR WORKOUT OF THE DAY I recommend you complete your workout in the morning. Consult pages 135–140 for an at-a-glance look at each routine. This will save you time as you exercise, preventing the need to constantly flip pages.

■ A DAILY MENU Each day you will find detailed meal suggestions. (Recipes for dishes with asterisks can be found in Chapter 6.) Although it is best that you follow this meal plan to a T, you may make strategic modifications if needed. Follow the advice in Chapter 4 if you choose to modify the daily menus, and always follow the A, B, C, D, E, and F nutritional rules.

- **AN INSPIRING SUCCESS STORY** Each day I've included a first-person account from a client who has successfully completed the two-week makeover. These clients reveal how they struggled and ultimately triumphed. I hope their stories provide the inspiration you need to stay on track.

- **AN EXCUSE BUSTER** For each day of the program, I've included a common excuse that I've heard from my clients as they completed this program—and my response to the excuse. In my more than 15 years of personal training, I've heard some pretty incredible excuses for not wanting to work out. These range from obscure sudden maladies, aches, and pains to cries that "It's that time of the month!" As I pride myself on having an inordinate amount of patience and the ability to sense when a client is offering a legitimate reason for not working out, I offer you the proper retorts, or excuse busters, if you will, to those excuses that may still be taking shape somewhere in your brain.

- **A DAILY JOURNAL** For each day, space is provided for you to write down your thoughts, feelings, and progress on the program. I suggest you write in your journal every day. If you don't like writing in this book, then keep your journal in a separate notebook or even on the computer. It doesn't matter where you write, just as long as you do it.

I suggest you start your program on a Monday. Before you start, however, make sure you have everything you need to ensure your success, including the following:

- Exercise clothing and shoes

- Exercise equipment, including stability ball, medicine ball, and dumbbells

- The right foods in your kitchen

- A "before" photo (This can serve as inspiration later, as you work to maintain your results.)

■ A record of your current measurements, weight, clothing sizes, and body fat percentage

Also, please do not start the makeover until you have read Chapters 1 through 4. The information in those chapters serves as the foundation for this program. Without it, you will feel lost and confused. Worse, you will not have built the motivation needed to stick with the program.

THE CARDIO-SCULPTING ROUTINE

Ball Tap

Ball Tap with Medicine Ball

Side Squat with Medicine Ball Wood Chop

Jogging in Place with Medicine Ball

Jumping Jacks with Shoulder Press

Jumping Jacks with Lateral Raises

Shadow Boxing with Dumbbells

Calf Raises with Dumbbell Presses

Squat Thrusts with Medicine Ball

Mountain Climbers with Medicine Ball

Push-Ups with
Stability Ball

Ball Tucks

Pike

Platypus Walk
with
Medicine Ball

Jumping
Lunges

Side Step Squat
with
Medicine ball

Low Plank on
Stability Ball

High Plank on
Stability Ball

Push-Ups to
T-Stands

Sumo Lunge
with Side Kick
and Frog Jump

Jump Squats

Reverse Lunge
with Front Kick

David's Dumbbell
Wraparound

David's Inverted
Dumbbell
Chest Press

Dumbbell Skull
Crushers on Ball

Incline Dumbbell Press
on Ball

Bench Dips on Ball

Reverse Plank

David's Ultimate
Shoulder Shaper I

David's Ultimate
Shoulder Shaper II

Hyperextensions

Wide Dumbbell Rows

Spiderman Push-Ups

Plyometric Push-Ups

Forward and
Reverse
Crossover
Lunges with
Biceps Curls

Plié Squat with
Concentration
Curl

Leg Scissors

Side Crunch on Ball

Concentrated
Crunch on
Ball with
Medicine Ball

Double Crunch
with Ball

THE ABS AND CORE ROUTINE

Good Mornings

Good Mornings with
Rotation

High Plank with
Stability Ball

David's Ultimate Torso
Crunch

Double Oblique
Crunch

Reverse Oblique
Crunch

Handoff

Mid Back
Hyperextensions
on Ball

Rear Deltoid
Laterals with
Medicine Ball

Lower Back
Challenge

THE LEGS AND BUTT ROUTINE

Leg Lift with
Medicine Ball

The Clam with
Medicine Ball

The Clam II with
Medicine Ball

Inner Thigh Raise

Reverse Prone
Scissors

Superman with
Medicine Ball

Donkey Kicks

Hydrants

Sissy Squats

Bridge with
Stability Ball

Hamstring Curls

One-Leg
Hamstring Curls

Pelvic Tilt

Butt Squeeze

Standing
Asymmetrical
Lunges

Irish Jig

Chest Opener

Shoulder
Stretch

Triceps Stretch

Groin Stretch

Wide Angle Stretch

Buttocks
Stretch

Thigh Stretch

Abdominal
Stretch

DAY 1

As with many things in our lives, starting something is the hardest thing to do. Today I want you to get up and say, "This is the start of the new me. I can and will make the most of my life. I will set out to change the one thing over which I have the most control—myself."

Today's Workout

- ■ The cardio sculpting routine

- ■ 45 minutes of additional cardio

Today's Menu

Breakfast:	Protein Shake
Midmorning Snack:	*Scrambled Egg Whites with Shiitake Mushrooms and Turkey Bacon
Lunch:	*Tuna Cobb Salad
Midafternoon snack:	Cup of *Vegetable Soup
Dinner:	Protein Shake or *Turkey Lasagna *and* Spinach

Excuse Buster

Excuse: "I am too tired to do my workout."

The Bust: Being tired shouldn't necessarily prevent you from working out, but rather, it might alter the type of exercise you do or the amount of time you spend doing it. When done correctly, exercise should stimulate you physically and mentally. Your workout will turn a day that is lacking in drive, motivation, and energy into one that is positively reinforcing and bursting with energy and excitement at the possibility of it all.

"By the time I met David as part of the 'Extreme Makeover' television show, I was willing to try anything. Although I thought I had a good knowledge of how to lose weight, I was willing to concede that my formula wasn't working and hadn't worked for a long time. I had always lifted weights at the gym, learning the exercises from bodybuilders and bodybuilding magazines. I didn't know it at the time, but I was doing a 'guy's' program—and it showed. I had been lifting like that for 10 years by the time I met David. I weighed 175 pounds and had 17-inch arms. I wanted to be strong, but I didn't want to look like a guy! I wanted a feminine hourglass shape, but I looked like a big block. I wore 36/32 pants. That's right. My waist was bigger than the length of my legs! Things were really getting sad, and I was in a funk.

"David told me to cut the dairy and carbs out of my diet and put me on a completely different exercise program. Near the end of the second week, I could already see dramatic changes. The diet kicked in, the workouts kicked in, and whatever was stored in my system started coming out. David motivated me, teaching me to think every day about being healthy and fit. I began thinking hard about the choices I was making, about what I was putting in my mouth and what I was doing with my time.

"David transformed my 175-pound, bulky, and blocky body into a size 6 body with a sexy shape. It's now a year later, and I've maintained my results. I'm sticking with David's maintenance plan. I now have a good base of principles to use when thinking about what to eat and how and when to exercise. I can't thank him enough."

My Journal

Use this space to write down how you feel emotionally and physically, what you eat, any challenges you are facing, and the time, duration, and intensity of your workout.

_____

_____

_____

_____

_____

_____

_____

_____

_____

_____

_____

_____

DAY 2

After the initial excruciating soreness upon awakening the morning of day 2, remember this: The extreme makeover process is an honoring process. Successful completion of the two-week program will not only reward you with a perkier butt but also empower you in a deep, spiritually rewarding, and ultimately long-lasting and meaningful way. The ultimate prize—knowing that you can accomplish anything you set your mind to—is available to you, and, yes, it is truly attainable.

Today's Workout

- The abs and core toning routine

- 45 minutes of additional cardio

Today's Menu

Breakfast:	Protein Shake
Midmorning Snack:	*Spinach and Broccoli Egg White Frittata *and* Turkey Sausage
Lunch:	*Asian BBQ Chicken Kabob with Thai Salsa
Midafternoon Snack:	*Tuna Salad with Whole Grain Mustard and Water Chestnuts *and* Broccoli
Dinner:	Protein Shake or *Spicy Wasabi Salmon Burger *and* Spinach

Excuse Buster

Excuse: "I can skip a day and won't really miss anything."

The Bust: The road to wellness is not paved with yesterday's accomplishments. Rather, one day leads to another, and each one helps lay the foundation or brickwork to a better you. You may not think you will miss anything, but you won't gain anything either. I like to think I spend my days moving forward, making the most out of every moment. Exercise is one of those things that just feels right. Every hour of every day you have a choice. Do you choose to move, or do you choose to sit still? The choice is yours. You don't have the luxury of many tomorrows. Now is the time to make a difference and really shake up your routine!

ULTIMATE SUCCESS

Name: Pamela Michaels
Residence: New York, New York
Occupation: Board president of several nonprofits and mother of five
Age: 51
Inches Lost: $1^1/_2$ inches from her waist, 2 inches from her hips, $^1/_2$ inch from her arms
Weight Lost: 5 pounds
Other Accomplishments: Dropped 8 percent body fat
Comments: Pam had been training with me for almost one year when she started the two-week program. Although she was already naturally lean, we were able to further reduce her trouble areas—hips, butt, and thighs. After the end of the program, she resumed her three to four days per week exercise regime and has continued to shape and reduce her frame, impressing all those around her.

"I've always been a relatively lean person, but now that I'm in my fifties and approaching menopause, I decided to get in the best shape of my life. I've read a lot about menopause. I know after I enter this stage of life, it will be much tougher to lose weight and get in shape. So I decided to face menopause as fit and lean as I possibly could.

"I had another ulterior motive. My 24-year-old daughter is a fashion designer. She sewed me a very unforgiving, nonstructured chiffon gown. I wanted to look good in the gown, but when I tried it on, the seams stretched tightly across my hips rather than falling in a straight line. My daughter said to me, 'Mom, I can't let you wear this.' After hearing that comment, I was determined to look good in that dress!

"This program clearly works. There's no question about it. I saw results within three days, which helped to keep me motivated. In just three days my pants fit better. That's pretty amazing. In just that short amount of time, my daughters began to notice and were already complimenting me on the changes taking place in my body. Within just seven days, my daughter who is the fashion designer couldn't believe it. I went to a second fitting, and the seams fell completely straight. My arms, which the dress left exposed, were nicely toned. I knew I could wear the dress with confidence, and I was only halfway to my goal.

"It's not so much the weight I lost that impresses me as much as how well my clothes fit. I feel so good about myself. I feel healthier and cleaner. It's as if I've been through a toxic flushing. My body, skin, and hair look better than they have in years. I recommend this program to anyone who wants to feel and look her best."

My Journal

Use this space to write down how you feel emotionally and physically, what you eat, any challenges you are facing, and the time, duration, and intensity of your workout.

_____

_____

_____

_____

_____

_____

DAY 3

Make exercise ritualistic, just like brushing your teeth or combing your hair. Just as you rise, brush your teeth, wash your face, and comb your hair, you should also exercise. Once it becomes part of your morning ritual, exercise will be one of those things that you just can't miss. Think of starting your day without brushing your teeth—yuck! That's not a very tasty proposition for you or for your partner, coworkers, or kids. Similarly, starting your day without some form of exercise or movement will leave you feeling lackluster, depleted of positive energy, and, if you're anything like me, absolutely cranky and moody.

Today's Workout

- The cardio sculpting routine

- 45 minutes of additional cardio

Today's Menu

Breakfast:	Protein Shake
Midmorning Snack:	*Low-Fat Egg Salad
Lunch:	*Almond Crusted Chicken
Midafternoon Snack:	*Turkey and Spinach Burger
Dinner:	Protein Shake or *Sesame Chicken Fingers *and* Spinach

Excuse Buster

The Excuse: "I'm getting too big from my exercise routine, and think I should just take a month off to reduce some size."

The Bust: Exercise will do many things, but making you bigger should not be one of them, unless that is your specific objective. My Ultimate New York

Body Plan is designed to tone and sculpt your muscles and reduce your body fat while increasing your stamina, energy, and overall wellness. The appropriate response to an exercise program that is not yielding the desired results is to examine the exercises you are doing to make sure the form, weight, and number of repetitions are all correct. If it's your legs that seem to be getting bigger, I would stay away from any squat motions and stick to lunges, kicks, and plyometric moves such as leaping lunges, jump squats, and squat thrusts. Increasing the repetitions and decreasing the weight may also prove useful. I have also found that those who suffer from overdevelopment in the quadriceps (front thigh region) are often just a little off with their form, specifically, the weight distribution on their feet when they perform squats or lunges. Keep your weight on your heels.

ULTIMATE SUCCESS

Name: Nicholas Samuel Shahid, III
Residence: New York, New York
Occupation: Creative director
Age: 63
Weight Lost: 14 pounds
Other Accomplishments: Shrunk 2 $\frac{1}{2}$ inches from his waist and 1$\frac{1}{2}$ inches from his chest.
Comments: After training at my facility for almost 14 years, Sam was getting a little skeptical as to whether he would finally drop that extra padding. After two weeks on the program, however, Sam impressed us all by losing 14 pounds! After years of being in an exercise rut, the program gave this 63-year-old a renewed sense of hope, youth, and vitality. Since the program ended three months ago, Sam has maintained and improved on his impressive results, losing an additional nine pounds for a total of 23 pounds.

"As a creative director who works in the fashion industry, I often find myself at photo shoots surrounded not only by food, but also by slender 18-year-old models. These shoots tend to last 10 days, and generally by the end I always promise myself that I will lose weight and get back in shape as soon as I return to New York. Well, like everything else in life, my promises to myself never turned into reality. With each shoot, I gained more weight. I felt bloated and disillusioned.

"When David mentioned his 14-day program to me, I thought, 'How hard could that be? It's just 14 days.' Well, I will be honest with you. It is hard. If you do it properly, it controls your life, at least in the beginning. I live alone and tend to eat out and socialize at night. I also live in the city and am literally surrounded by food. By the third day of the program, I felt as if everyone was eating. The temptation was overwhelming. It seemed as if I smelled and saw food everywhere I turned. I stayed in at night, and my evenings felt very long to me. I missed my old lifestyle.

"But something interesting happened during the course of the two-week program. After I began seeing results, I forgot about the pain and reversed the control. Instead of the diet controlling me, I controlled the diet. After the last day of the program, I planned to go out to dinner and celebrate. I dreamed of drinking wine and eating pasta—breaking almost every one of David's nutritional rules during one long, decadent meal. Well, when I got to the restaurant, I ended up ordering a wine spritzer and fish instead of pasta. I was amazed that I could enjoy myself at dinner and have only three-quarters of a glass of wine.

"The great thing about this program is that you do see results. You feel great about yourself by the end of the program. My pants are just falling off me. I am going on holiday at the end of the summer and will look to the program for a two-week refresher to get me ready for the beach."

My Journal

Use this space to write down how you feel emotionally and physically, what you eat, any challenges you are facing, and the time, duration, and intensity of your workout.

DAY 4

An automobile needs premium fuel to operate at its highest potential. So does your body. Fuel, whether in the form of a protein-rich meal or a delicious and nutritious meal replacement shake, is the key to extreme body transformations.

Today's Workout

- ■ The legs and butt toning routine

- ■ 45 minutes of additional cardio

Today's Menu

Breakfast:	Protein Shake
Midmorning Snack:	Hard-Boiled Egg
Lunch:	*Fennel Crusted Salmon
Midafternoon Snack:	*Low-Fat Chicken Salad
Dinner:	Protein Shake or *Turkey Lasagna *and* Spinach

Excuse Buster

The Excuse: "I deserve to eat those chocolate chip cookies because I've been working so hard."

The Bust: When my clients, or someone else for that matter, tell me that they deserve to eat some snack (whether it is cookies, pizza, or ice cream) because they've been working so hard, I respond with a question: "Why do you look at those foods as rewards?" I would rather reward myself with something delicious, nutritious, and wholesome, such as raw nuts, fresh fruit, or an occasional piece of dark chocolate. Hard work should be rewarded, not punished by adding calories and fat that will negate everything that we've just worked so hard to achieve. We need to change our mind-set and start looking for the sound reward. To me, the ultimate reward is in looking in the mirror and knowing that I look as good as I can and that I feel good too .

ULTIMATE SUCCESS

Name: Danielle Narov
Residence: Queens, New York
Occupation: High school student
Age: 16
Weight Lost: 7 pounds
Other Accomplishments: Reduced body fat percentage by almost 10 percent. Lost 5 inches from her waist.
Comments: One would think that being on the tennis team would be all the athletics this 16-year-old girl would need. Her poor diet caused her to carry more fat around her midsection than she needed. She also lacked the strength and stamina to really excel on the tennis court. Within two weeks she had lost the baby fat and added enough strength to do push-ups (on her toes, not her knees). She is knocking the tennis ball all over the court now. Danielle continues to exercise with intensity by doing my boot camp video three to four times per week.

"Even though I play tennis for my school, I had become extremely out of shape. I knew my body was flabby, and I didn't like the way I looked. My sister's bat mitzvah was coming up, and I wanted to look good for the event. I had heard about David's program and decided to give it a try.

"When I first met with David and told him about my expectations, he mentioned that I might not be able to lose as much fat as I wanted in just 14 days. Well, I'm happy to say that I reduced my waist by over 5 inches. That's just crazy!

"Because I was so out of shape, I felt very sore after my first few work-outs. That soreness soon went away. The rest of the program went smoothly for me. I easily stuck with the nutrition plan. My only challenge was fitting the prescribed amount of exercise into each day. As a student, I have a number of tasks I must complete each day after school. Some days it was hard to fit in those tasks, my homework, and my exercise and still get to bed at a reasonable hour.

"I'm so happy with my results. I lost a ton of fat and built a lot of muscle. I'm very happy with the way I look. The only part that's bittersweet is that my favorite pair of pants no longer fits."

My Journal

Use this space to write down how you feel emotionally and physically, what you eat, any challenges you are facing, and the time, duration, and intensity of your workout.

_____

_____

_____

_____

_____

_____

_____

_____

_____

_____

DAY 5

The phrase "Stay in the moment" will never take on more importance than it will today and every day during this program. With only 14 days to sculpt, tone, and burn, there is no room for complacence or daydreaming.

Today's Workout

- ■ The abdomen and core toning routine

- ■ 45 minutes of additional cardio

Today's Menu

Breakfast:	Protein Shake
Midmorning Snack:	*Scrambled Egg Whites with Ground Turkey and Chopped Tomatoes
Lunch:	*Chicken and Shiitake Mushroom Burger *and* *Bok Choy with Red Peppers and Almonds
Midafternoon Snack:	*Tomato Soup *and* *Tuna Salad with Whole Grain Mustard and Water Chestnuts
Dinner:	Protein Shake or *Salmon Cake *and* Spinach

Excuse Buster

The Excuse: "My boyfriend/girlfriend bought me the ice cream; how could I say no?"

The Bust: Passive junk food bingeing (also known as secondhand eating) is very destructive. You are in control, and no one can make you eat anything. Where did that kind of thinking get Adam and Eve? Get my point? We have the power to control our own fate and destiny. Do not relinquish that power to anyone for any reason.

"Ever since I can remember, I've had an unhealthy relationship with food. I loved dining out with friends, but when I ate out, I tended to overeat.

"I will be honest. The two-week makeover was tough for me. I had to turn my back on my old, destructive relationship with food and welcome a new concept into my life. Instead of enjoying food, food became fuel. Food became what I ate to power my workouts and my work life.

"To avoid temptation, I sequestered myself in my home every night. During those first 14 days, I didn't trust myself enough to eat out at a restaurant. I really missed the social atmosphere of restaurant eating, but I knew I could make it for 14 days. As time went on, each day of the program began to take on a familiar routine. I'll admit that I hated the routine at first, but after 14 days, it became a natural part of my life.

"I got to an amazing place fitnesswise during the 14 days. I had never done that much cardio in my life. I was the type of person who warmed up for 10 minutes on the treadmill before heading for my toning workout. Now I'm doing 45 minutes of cardio almost every day, and I love it. I love training really hard, and how it makes me feel.

"On my last day of the program, my friends were all giving me high fives and congratulating me on my progress and dedication. It was an amazing high. This program has taught me a lot about nutrition and fitness that I will be incorporating into my life. I feel as if my body is a brand new car—as if I have shiny new insides that are very precious to me. I think twice about everything I put in my mouth because I don't want to ruin all my hard work. I have a set of rules to guide my eating at home. Even though I no longer am officially on the program, I'm still sticking to the rules. I don't think I'll be pigging out for a very long time. The program is 100 percent doable. If I can do it, anyone can."

My Journal
Use this space to write down how you feel emotionally and physically, what you eat, any challenges you are facing, and the time, duration, and intensity of your workout.

_____

_____

_____

_____

_____

_____

DAY 6

Sculpting your butt requires you to put your brain in your butt! It may seem very rudimentary and quite silly, but I guarantee that with that mind-body connection, you will see the "bigger"(and I don't mean fatter) picture, allowing you to feel, sculpt, and melt away those unwanted inches not just in your butt, but throughout your entire body.

Today's Workout

■ The cardio sculpting routine

■ 45 minutes of additional cardio

Today's Menu

Breakfast:	Protein Shake
Midmorning Snack:	*Roasted Red Pepper Frittata
Lunch:	*Mustard Crusted Halibut *and* Mesclun Salad
Midafternoon Snack:	*Vegetable Soup
Dinner:	Protein Shake or *Asian Style Salmon with *Spinach and Shiitake Mushroom Stir-Fry

Excuse Buster

The Excuse: "One piece of bread isn't going to kill me."

The Bust: One piece of bread or one cookie may not kill you, but it definitely won't help you either. Think of yourself as a high-powered machine, one that needs the purest, most premium fuel to function. On a more scientific note, bread is just empty calories, broken down by your body as sugar and stored as fat. What's the point? You're working too hard to do bread!

"I originally signed up as a participant on the 'Extreme Makeover' show because I wanted a dermatologist to turn back the clock and remove the sun-damaged skin from my face. At the time, I didn't think too much about what I wanted for my body, although I am in my mid-40s and as soon as you hit 40 it becomes harder and harder to maintain your weight.

"When David first saw me, he said I could lose a little weight but that he wanted to put the main focus on building muscle tone. Until that time I had been pretty active. I played tennis two to three times a week, walked regularly, and did a free weight routine at the gym. I have a college degree in physical education, so I felt as if I knew what I was doing.

"I soon learned that I didn't know as much as I thought. David is a true genius at being able to combine several facets of exercise into one efficient motion. His routines include not one second of wasted time or energy. Many of his exercises combine upper and lower body movements with the cardio so you are getting more bang for every minute that you exercise.

"In addition to revolutionizing the way I worked out, David also helped me to make a few crucial changes to my diet. I learned how to eat better protein and carbohydrate foods. I loved his protein shakes and, in particular, his turkey chili recipe. In Texas, it's almost a sacrilege to make chili with turkey instead of beef, but I'd rather eat that turkey chili 21 days in a row than eat a burger at this point. Of course, I don't tell my friends I put turkey in the chili—unless they ask.

"I lost over 10 percent of my body fat within two weeks on David's program. It's been a year since I worked with David, and I've maintained my results the entire time. Although I have not been able to check my body fat, my clothes still fit perfectly. I think the most important lesson I've learned is that there's never an excuse to cheat. There is always a time and always a place to exercise. Instead of thinking to myself, 'I deserve to have that piece of chocolate,' I now think, 'I deserve to be thin and say no to that chocolate.'"

My Journal

Use this space to write down how you feel emotionally and physically, what you eat, any challenges you are facing, and the time, duration, and intensity of your workout.

_____

_____

_____

_____

_____

_____

_____

_____

DAY 7

Sculpting and toning your body takes on a major significance when you look at the big picture. Extreme life transformations are physical, emotional, psychological, and spiritual. You must transform on all levels to successfully complete this program.

Today's Workout

- The legs and butt toning routine

- 45 minutes of additional cardio

Today's Menu

Breakfast:	Protein Shake
Midmorning Snack:	*Low-Fat Egg Salad
Lunch:	*Mediterranean Chicken Stir-Fry
Midafternoon Snack:	Fresh Roasted Turkey Breast
Dinner:	Protein Shake or *Tuna and Shrimp Kabob

Excuse Buster

The Excuse: "My boss is giving me a really hard time at work; therefore, I need this oatmeal cookie."

The Bust: Not that long ago, a very dear friend of mine was stressing over a relationship that was causing him much unhappiness, which resulted in bingeing and too many vodka gimlets. My advice after hours of counseling was simple: "Don't give anyone the power to control your happiness." The same advice applies in this situation. You are engaging in an incredibly challenging but rewarding program. The power, energy, and focus are all in you. Do not relinquish that control by giving in to weak impulses brought on by the stress caused by another. With a strong resolve you will stay the course and emerge a winner.

Name: Amy Larocca

Residence: New York, New York

Occupation: Magazine editor

Age: 28

Weight Lost: 8 pounds

Other Accomplishments: Shrunk her back circumference by $1\frac{1}{2}$ inches, her waist by 2 inches, and her thighs by $\frac{1}{2}$ inch. She dropped from a size 8 to a size 4.

Comments: As an editor for a major weekly magazine in New York, Amy must attend plenty of dinners and parties, and she never has enough time for exercise and eating properly. That being said, Amy was incredibly disciplined and focused during the program. A few months after she completed the program, we ate dinner together. She looked even better and had continued to adhere to the diet and exercise tenets of the program.

"Like any girl, I always thought I needed to lose 10 pounds. Although I've never been overweight, I always felt I could be a bit fitter and more trim. My body weight and fitness level have varied, depending on my work schedule and how stressful life becomes. There have been times when I've been really fit, and times that I definitely have not. I know what being fit feels like, and I also know when it eludes me.

"I decided to try David's two-week makeover because I had heard a lot about him. Specifically, I had heard that he's really tough. I knew he would make me work hard, and that's what I knew I needed to get in shape. The program didn't let me down. It's wonderful.

"The fitness and nutrition components are definitely challenging. There were times that I really wanted to eat a piece of bread. There were times in the beginning when I was really sore. The soreness and cravings soon gave way. Within a short period of time, I discovered muscles that I didn't even know I had. Although I resisted the protein shakes at first, they grew on me. Now, I look forward to them, and if I don't have one on a given day, I miss it.

"My carbohydrate cravings have diminished greatly as well. By the end of the program, I felt so much more energized. I loved that I had persevered and pushed myself every day. I felt such a strong sense of accomplishment. Most important, I learned a lot about fitness and nutrition that I can take with me and continue on my own. For example, I realized that I can—and should— push myself harder. I lost those last 10 pounds, and I feel fantastic."

My Journal

Use this space to write down how you feel emotionally and physically, what you eat, any challenges you are facing, and the time, duration, and intensity of your workout.

_____

_____

_____

_____

_____

_____

_____

_____

_____

_____

_____

_____

DAY 8

Seven days down, and seven to go. You are halfway to the new you. Can you see it, feel it, and taste it? The answer should be a resounding yes to all the above. The soreness should be dissipating and being replaced by a newfound energy source and confidence deep inside you.

Today's Workout

- The cardio sculpting routine

- 45 minutes of additional cardio

Today's Menu

Breakfast:	Protein Shake
Midmorning Snack:	Egg Whites with Turkey Sausage
Lunch:	*Curried Almond Striped Bass
Midafternoon Snack:	Raw Almonds
Dinner:	Protein Shake or *Chicken and Eggplant Wrap

Excuse Buster

The Excuse: "The milk in my latte doesn't really count as dairy, does it?"

The Bust: Even seemingly innocent things like a latte (which is half milk) will definitely add up on the fat and calorie fronts. If you must have a latte (and I'm not thrilled about the consumption of coffee), then please halve the amount and switch to skim milk. In this case, skim milk is definitely a sounder choice. Having said that, you will not be consuming any dairy (remember the A, B, C, D, E, and F) during this two-week program. Perhaps that will be your first treat (or one might say cheat) upon successful completion of the program.

ULTIMATE SUCCESS

Name: Deborah Schindler
Residence: New York, New York
Occupation: Film and television producer
Age: 47
Weight Lost: 9 pounds
Other Accomplishments: Dropped 9 percent body fat and shrunk her bust by 2 $\frac{1}{2}$ inches, her waist by 4 inches, and her hips by 2 $\frac{1}{2}$ inches.
Comments: Deborah needed to be reintroduced to exercise, having not been doing anything physical for more than a year. We had also decided for scheduling reasons to train her and her husband (Todd Thaler) together. To some extent, this was an added challenge because they were not necessarily on the same fitness level. After a somewhat slow beginning, Deborah experienced impressive results. Her back, which had been an issue (she had had back surgery two years prior for a ruptured disk), is now more stable and stronger.

"My husband and I both work full time and have a teenage daughter and many household responsibilities. Over the years, I've often pushed exercise to the side as I focused on my family and career. Now that I'm in my 40s, however, that tactic was beginning to catch up to me. I embarked on David's program to get in shape and make fitness a priority in my life.

"Because I hadn't exercised before, the first few days of the program were tough. On days 2 and 3, I was pretty sore. The nutrition plan was also an adjustment. Our social and family life revolved around dinner. It was hard to drink a shake at 7 instead of having our usual sit-down meal at 7:30 or 8 P.M. That was a big change. I also had to give up my ritual of a 10 P.M. snack with this program, which was hard to do.

"The program menu included many delicious meals, so that helped to make up for it. The results, after two weeks, also made it worthwhile. My body shape changed. My body fat percentage dropped from 32 percent to 23 percent. All my clothes fit more loosely around the waist.

"Since the program ended, I've kept up my exercise. I actually crave my daily cardio. I'm also eating smaller, more frequent meals, and I've traded that 10 P.M. snack for a cup of chamomile tea. If you are considering starting the program or are somewhere in the middle of it, be persistent and keep your eye on the goal. If you follow the program, you will achieve indisputable, amazing results."

My Journal
Use this space to write down how you feel emotionally and physically, what you eat, any challenges you are facing, and the time, duration, and intensity of your workout.

DAY 9

I often say, "Less is more." In fact, I have tried to base my life on this saying. As this program is short on time but long on demands and expectations, optimizing the time spent is essential. We will choose to do those things that matter most: following the strict precepts and guidelines of the food and training regimens and complementing them by living a spiritually sounder and more balanced life.

Today's Workout

- ■ The abs and core toning routine

- ■ 45 minutes of additional cardio

Today's Menu

Breakfast:	Protein Shake
Midmorning Snack:	*Scrambled Egg Whites with Shiitake Mushrooms and Turkey Bacon
Lunch:	*Chicken Meatballs with Tomato Eggplant Sauce
Midafternoon Snack:	*Seared Tuna Burger *and* Spinach
Dinner:	Protein Shake or *Sesame Chicken Fingers with *Pureed Broccoli and Roasted Red Peppers

Excuse Buster

The Excuse: "The cookies and ice cream are low in fat, so I can eat more."

The Bust: When discussing food consumption, one must do both a quantitative and a qualitative analysis. I am almost loath to say this, but I would rather you eat one regular cookie with a tablespoon of ice cream instead of four low-fat cookies and a greater quantity of low-fat ice cream. If some is good, more isn't necessarily better.

Name: Todd Thaler
Residence: New York, New York
Occupation: Casting director
Age: 47
Weight Lost: 10 pounds
Other Accomplishments: Shrunk his waist 3 inches
Comments: Training with his wife, Deborah, presented a challenge at first, but once we found the balance, we were off to the races. Todd carried his excess fat in his midsection and obliques. By increasing the cardiovascular exercise and adding lightweight resistance training, we brought about impressive results. He's pumped and staying focused on losing more weight, fat, and inches. In fact, seven weeks after completing the program, Todd has continued his hard work and dropped an additional inch from his waist.

"Last year I spent five months in southern Louisiana filming *Because of Winn-Dixie*. Each day I ate po' boys, fried oysters, and lots of thick-sauced Southern cooking. I also took many liberties with the set food. There's always a good selection of healthy foods on the set, but also plenty of candy bars, cake, and doughnuts. By the time I returned to New York, I had gained 13 pounds and had graduated from a size 33 to a size 35 waist jeans.

"Not only did I hope David's two-week program would help me eliminate the spare tire I had developed during the shoot, but I also wanted to get back into a regular exercise routine. It worked. I'm now exercising every day and doing some yoga in the mornings. Even more important, I lost 10 pounds. That's an amazing amount of weight to lose in just two weeks. I'm now wearing size 34 jeans, with my belt on the last hole. I haven't been on the last hole of my belt for at least a year.

"In addition to the weight I lost, David's program also helped me to develop my upper body. I have a concave sternum, something I've always been self-conscious about. With my newly developed chest, arms, and shoulders, I now feel confident wearing tank tops in public.

"The program was definitely challenging. I had my moments when I was in a funk, but I never cheated. I either cooked or ordered in for my teenage daughter in the evenings, and it was very difficult to watch her eat mashed potatoes or rice while I drank my shake for dinner.

"Even though the nutritional part of the program was challenging, I have developed new habits that I know I will keep for a lifetime. For example, instead of a sandwich for lunch, I'm more likely to eat a salad with grilled chicken. Instead of a bagel with cream cheese for breakfast, I now have yogurt or cottage cheese. You have to have real discipline to stick to the program, but the miraculous thing is that the results are so amazing. This program really works."

My Journal
Use this space to write down how you feel emotionally and physically, what you eat, any challenges you are facing, and the time, duration, and intensity of your workout.

THE ULTIMATE NEW YORK BODY PLAN

DAY 10

You're almost there. I'm sure you're already seeing some light at the end of the proverbial tunnel. Now is the time to really step it up and give it all you have. Can you add more cardiovascular exercise to the program or push out those additional repetitions when doing lunges, push-ups, or crunches? Programs this intense require you to push yourself beyond your preconceived limits.

Today's Workout

- ▨ The cardio sculpting routine

- ▨ 45 minutes of additional cardio

Today's Menu

Breakfast:	Protein Shake
Midmorning Snack:	*Scrambled Egg Whites with Shiitake Mushrooms and Turkey Bacon
Lunch:	*Chicken Meatballs with Tomato Eggplant Sauce
Midafternoon Snack:	*Seared Tuna Burger *and* Spinach
Dinner:	Protein Shake or *Sesame Chicken Fingers with *Pureed Broccoli and Roasted Red Peppers

Excuse Buster

The Excuse: "I don't need my cardio exercise today. I spent most of my day shopping at the mall."

The Bust: Unless you were doing laps through the lingerie department followed by lunges down the skin-care aisle, you had better do some cardiovascular exercise after you've unloaded the packages. You need 45 minutes to an hour of cardio every day. Fourteen days is not that long. Stay the course.

"I've been training on a regular basis for 10 years and was already in pretty good shape. When I heard about David's program, I decided to see just how fit and how ripped I could get.

"The first three days were the most difficult. David spaced my meals about three hours apart, with my last solid meal around 6 or 6: 30 P.M. This virtually eliminated my social life for two weeks, as I could not go out to dinner at night or out for a drink. Yet, I knew I could hang in there for just two weeks.

"The exercise program was difficult. There's no question about that. During the first few days, my body was completely exhausted. Once I began to adjust to the exercise and nutrition regimens, however, I found it easier to get up in the morning. I'd wake up with more energy, and I didn't have to pound a couple cups of coffee at 2 to 3 P.M. to keep myself awake. I felt alert all day long.

"Now that the official program is over, I'm still sticking with many of its tenets. I still eat ground turkey and egg whites for breakfast and a small piece of meat with a salad for lunch. For dinner, I do go out to eat, but I always order something low in carbohydrates and fat.

"In addition to cutting my body fat percentage nearly in half, the program helped me to cut back on my cigarette habit. It was mostly a survival mechanism. I was so tired of gasping for air during my workouts with David that I had to cut back. It's now my plan to quit altogether by my birthday, which is less than a month away. I'm headed to Miami in a couple weeks, and that will be the true litmus test of the program—to see how great I look on the beach."

My Journal

Use this space to write down how you feel emotionally and physically, what you eat, any challenges you are facing, and the time, duration, and intensity of your workout.

_____

_____

_____

_____

_____

_____

_____

_____

_____

_____

DAY 11

Remember the ultimate rules of nutrition. I know you've been following the meal plan, including the meal replacement powder and the daily vitamins and minerals, but don't leave anything to chance. Make sure you are watching your sodium intake and staying hydrated. Drinking sufficient amounts of water is an essential part of this program and will assist your body as it gets rid of toxins and other impurities.

Today's Workout

- The legs and butt toning routine

- 45 minutes of additional cardio

Today's Menu

Breakfast:	Protein Shake
Midmorning Snack:	*Mushroom and Asparagus Frittata
Lunch:	*Stuffed Red Pepper with Ground Turkey
Midafternoon Snack:	*Turkey Lasagna
Dinner:	Protein Shake or *Low-Fat Chicken Salad *and* Spinach

Excuse Buster

The Excuse: "I'm too sore from my last workout to do anything today."

The Bust: Soreness from a previous day's workout is not a good reason to skip today's session. In fact, muscle soreness is due primarily to lactic acid buildup. Often the best response to this type of soreness is muscle movement through exercise. Movement, proper hydration, and nutrition are the perfect remedies for soreness and should keep you motivated, mobile, and productive. If you really want to pamper yourself and continue to move forward in the right direction, sign up for a massage—and keep your exercise appointment intact.

Name: Bonnie Berkovits

Residence: New York, New York

Occupation: Customer care manager

Age: 46

Weight Lost: 10 pounds

Other Accomplishments: Shrunk 3 inches from her waist, 4 $1/2$ inches from her bust, 3 inches from her hips, 1 inch from her thighs, and $1/2$ inch from her arms.

Comments: With a classic apple-shaped body, Bonnie needed to lose about 40 pounds. We knew we couldn't accomplish that in just two weeks. Also, with little exercise experience under her belt, the program started a little tediously. She was steadfast in her determination to "handle" all that I presented to her. Unlike some of my other clients, she welcomed the diet and did not feel deprived at all. After years of yo-yo dieting, she is finally on the way to achieving her fitness goals.

"I have always had an unhealthy relationship with food and exercise—well, let's just say that I've never been an exercise junkie. When I was asked to participate in David's two-week program, I saw this as my chance to finally get my butt in gear! No longer was I going to start training or eating well 'tomorrow'—I was and am ready to live in the present.

"I've worked with a therapist for the past two years, trying to open myself up to feeling again. I told David I felt ready to finally lose the extra 40 pounds I had gained during the past 10 years and to change my diet for the better. I wanted to feel good about myself, and be able to wear a bikini again.

"The program was actually very easy for me, and the two weeks of working out with David helped me as much as my time with my therapist. I never deviated from the diet. I'll admit, I didn't always fit in all of the cardio David wanted me to do each day, which makes my results that much more impressive. I dropped almost 10 percent body fat. You can't imagine the changes I'm seeing in my body. I feel great. I'm more energetic.

"I have size 12s, 10s, and 8s in my closet, and I can now get into a few of my 8s that haven't fit in a long, long time. I look good and I feel so much better about myself. I feel as if I've been given another opportunity at life. I'm approaching my forty-seventh birthday, and I'm tired of living on the sidelines. I'm taking it to the 100 yard line."

My Journal
Use this space to write down how you feel emotionally and physically, what you eat, any challenges you are facing, and the time, duration, and intensity of your workout.

_____

_____

_____

_____

_____

_____

_____

_____

_____

_____

_____

DAY 12

I know you're liking what you see, but that doesn't mean there are no more lessons to learn. Don't start patting yourself on the back yet. If you've already attained your goals, set another goal today to exceed them. Complacency leads to lethargy and lethargy to disappointment and failure. Stay sharp, stay focused, and keep your eye on the prize: your transformed body. That should be enough incentive and motivation to take you through the next 48 hours of the program.

Today's Workout

- The cardio sculpting routine

- 45 minutes of additional cardio

Today's Menu

Breakfast:	Protein Shake
Midmorning Snack:	*Scrambled Egg Whites with Ground Turkey and Chopped Tomatoes
Lunch:	*Asian BBQ Chicken Kabob with Thai Salsa
Midafternoon Snack:	*Spicy Wasabi Salmon Burger *and* Broccoli
Dinner:	Protein Shake or *Striped Bass with Mint Parsley Pesto

Excuse Buster

The Excuse: "I've got a horrible hangover, and the thought of doing any exercise is nauseating me."

The Bust: Why were you drinking in the first place? Never mind, nobody's perfect, but, my friend, as they say, you've got to pay if you're going to play.

At the risk of sounding totally cruel and heartless: *Get your lazy butt out of bed!* The first step will be the hardest, but once you're out of bed, the rest will be a breeze. As your punishment (yes, drinking is definitely taboo), you must complete 15 to 30 additional minutes of cardiovascular exercise. If I were you, I probably wouldn't jump around a lot, but I would work up a good sweat. Make sure to hydrate with lots of water (even more than you would ordinarily drink) and take plenty of vitamins, minerals, and, in particular, milk thistle to cleanse your liver. When all is said and done, you will be a sweaty mess, but you will definitely have worked toward ridding yourself of the alcohol in your body.

ULTIMATE SUCCESS

Name: Galaxia Barraza
Residence: New York, New York
Occupation: Mom, public relations and casting specialist
Weight Lost: 9 pounds
Other Accomplishments: Shrunk her waist by 4 1/2 inches and her thighs and hips by 1 inch. Dropped 8 percent body fat.
Comments: Gali had given birth to a baby girl just four months before starting the program and had not exercised before, during, or since the pregnancy. We definitely had our work cut out for us. Building up her cardiovascular stamina and strength endurance were key components to her success. By the end of the program, Gali could exercise aerobically for 45 minutes to an hour and had switched from her usual diet of rice and potatoes to one of vegetables, chicken, fish, salads, and protein shakes.

"I gained a lot of weight when I was pregnant—59 pounds. Before then, I had been naturally thin and wore size 0 clothing. I never watched what I ate, nor did I exercise. I didn't have to. During my pregnancy, however, I craved sweets and gave into my temptations.

"After giving birth, I figured I would never lose the excess weight I had gained. Then I heard about David's program. The first couple of days were really hard—really hard. I felt so sore, and I thought I wasn't going to make it, but David told me it would go away. He was right. By day 3 I felt great.

"Adjusting to the diet was also a challenge. Before the program I ate only carbs. Often, for dinner, I would eat potatoes and rice. I also ate late, after 10 P.M. On the program, there are almost no carbs, and you're supposed to eat your last meal by 7 P.M. Although this certainly was an adjustment for me, the food was really good, and my cravings for carbs went away after three to four days.

"I feel great and am almost back to my prepregnancy weight. I used to wear a size 0, and I don't think I will get that small again. That's fine with me. I'm now a size 4, and I am happy. A lot of people look at me and say incredulously, 'You had a baby?'"

My Journal

Use this space to write down how you feel emotionally and physically, what you eat, any challenges you are facing, and the time, duration, and intensity of your workout.

_____

_____

_____

_____

_____

_____

_____

_____

DAY 13

Your clothes are fitting better, you have more energy than you've had in years, and you're motivated to push harder and stay the course even after this program is over. If you agree and can relate to these sentiments, then challenge yourself further by adding an additional 30 to 45 minutes of cardiovascular exercise to your regimen. You are on your way to completing the 14-day program with flying colors, and it will definitely be easier than it was last week.

Today's Workout

- The abs and core toning routine

- 45 minutes of additional cardio

Today's Menu

Breakfast:	Protein Shake
Midmorning Snack:	*Low-Fat Egg Salad
Lunch:	*Flounder with Arugula Almond Pesto
Midafternoon Snack:	*Tomato Soup *and* Turkey Sausage
Dinner:	Protein Shake or *Chicken and Shiitake Mushroom Burger and *Ratatouille

Excuse Buster

The Excuse: "It's that time of the month, and I can't get out of bed."

The Bust: I grew up with five women—three sisters, my mother, and my grandmother. I know all about that time of the month. I also know that it's no excuse to skip a workout. I'll accept that women's experiences vary, but I have seen the benefits of exercise here too. I would recommend sticking with this program during this time period (no pun intended). Exercise can help minimize the cramps associated with one's menstrual cycle. That along with lots of hydration and good vitamin, mineral, and herb supplementation will make that monthly occurrence less debilitating. I mean no disrespect and do not mean to trivialize this natural fact of life, but having worked with woman of all ages for 16 years, I have seen my clients rise above and conquer this monthly occurrence.

ULTIMATE SUCCESS

Name: Kenny Sylvester
Residence: New York, New York
Occupation: Managing director of the Red Eye Grille
Weight Lost: 10 pounds
Other Accomplishments: Shrunk his waist by 2 $\frac{1}{2}$ inches and gained an inch in his chest. Lost 8.5 percent body fat.
Comments: As a restaurant manager, Kenny is surrounded by bad food choices. He also works horrendous hours, staying at work until 3 A.M. quite often. He had not exercised since college. At more than 6 feet tall, he was not as fit as he appeared. By the end of the program, however, he was looking pretty spiffy in his suits.

"I went to the doctor one day and found out I had high blood pressure. My doctor told me that the excess weight I had gained during my wife's pregnancy (it was as if we were both eating for two) could be to blame. I'm one of those guys who, on the first of every month, says he's going to get back to the gym but who never does. Now that my health seemed to be suffering as a result, I decided to get serious about exercising and healthful eating. I had heard about David's program and decided to give it a try.

"Although the program was certainly challenging, it was easier than I expected. I've worked in the restaurant business for many years and have come to expect the food I eat to taste good. I've never eaten 'diet' food, and I expected the food on the program to taste like sawdust or wood with very little flavor. The food on the program was great. I was really impressed with the flavor. It tasted nothing like sawdust!

"I admit, I was tempted by the food that I see day in and day out at the restaurant, but I never gave in to the temptations except for two strawberries one night—hey, I'm human. The program actually felt like a detox for me. I am so used to eating on the run and grabbing any type of junk food that will stop the hunger. While on the program, for the first time in many years, I ate nutritious foods every day.

"My results were, of course, incredible. This was the perfect program for me. I'm wearing suits that I haven't been able to wear in 18 months. I've turned so many people in my restaurant on to this program. I'm a real believer."

My Journal

Use this space to write down how you feel emotionally and physically, what you eat, any challenges you are facing, and the time, duration, and intensity of your workout.

_____

_____

_____

_____

_____

_____

_____

DAY 14

Congratulations! By the end of the day, you will have successfully completed the two-week Ultimate New York Body Plan. During the past 13 days, you have displayed an inordinate amount of willpower, strength, and confidence. Oh yeah, you also look pretty fierce in that bikini and those jeans that didn't fit a couple of weeks ago. All that said, don't lose sight of the true importance of this program. This program will set you apart, enrich and empower your life like nothing before has done. The real reward gained through this program goes way beyond jeans and bikinis (not that those goals aren't rewarding). Embracing wellness as a lifelong partner is the ultimate goal and the invaluable prize.

Today's Workout

- ■ The cardio sculpting routine
- ■ 45 minutes of additional cardio

Today's Menu

Breakfast:	Protein Shake
Midmorning Snack:	*Scrambled Egg Whites with Shiitake Mushrooms and Turkey Bacon
Lunch:	*Shrimp on Cabbage Bed with Mustard Dressing Salad
Midafternoon Snack:	*Low-Fat Chicken Salad *and* Spinach
Dinner:	Protein Shake or *Middle Eastern Chicken Kabob with *Pureed Broccoli and Roasted Red Peppers

Excuse Buster

The Excuse: "I had a crisis at home, and there was no time to exercise today."

The Bust: The perfect response to a personal crisis is a little exercise. It all goes back to the concept that exercise should be ritualistic. Don't find reasons and excuses not to exercise, but rather respond to the crisis with an appropriate workout. This might mean getting out and taking a brisk walk around the block to clear your head. Action, not inaction, is the key to managing crises. My father embraced this philosophy and instilled this empowering belief in me. I want you to go forward and meet every challenge with a strong, positive response. Act, don't react, and don't lose sight of the power and wonder of you!

ULTIMATE SUCCESS

Name: Heidi Klum
Residence: New York, New York
Occupation: Supermodel, Supermom
Accomplishments: Heidi started working out again just four weeks after giving birth to her beautiful daughter. With safe, carefully focused, and custom-tailored sessions, we were able to get Heidi looking and feeling amazingly beautiful in just two weeks. What can I say that hasn't already been said about Heidi? She is the walking embodiment of the Sound Mind Sound Body principles.

"I didn't work out during my pregnancy, but since I've gone back to work pretty quickly after having my daughter, I have started working out with David again, a few days a week. I gained about 30 pounds during my pregnancy, but mostly around the stomach; my arms, legs, and face stayed pretty much my usual size.

"I wasn't worried so much about getting back in shape. My main concern was and is being healthy so I can take care of my daughter; she's definitely my first priority now. At the same time, I am a model, and I was scheduled to do my first photo shoot for my clothing line just a couple of months after having the baby. So the two-week program made a lot of sense. I have to say that I didn't follow the plan that strictly. I'm breast-feeding, and the most important thing to me is that I'm getting enough nutrients and that I'm fully energized, so I pass all that along!

"I do love the protein shakes, and I have been going to the gym a few days a week to exercise, but I'm using moderation. I eat sensibly, and I rest when I can and work out lightly. It's actually not recommended to exercise until at least six weeks after you give birth, so I guess you could say I was on a modified version of the two-week plan. I definitely saw results very quickly, even with the amount that I did do. I went to a fitting for a gorgeous dress to wear to the CFDA Awards event just five weeks after giving birth. By the time the event rolled around a week later, I was already smaller, and the dress had to be taken in at the last fitting.

"I don't honestly love working out, but I do it because I know it's good for me, that it's necessary in my line of work, and that it does give me an energized, positive feeling afterward. It's the getting there that's tough!

"I think I have pretty good nutrition and fitness habits, and actually, it's my lifestyle in general. I don't go overboard with anything. I eat what I want, but not loads of anything unhealthy. And I exercise when I can, but not every single day or when I'm exhausted.

"I love working with David because he knows all this about me. He can help me tailor a program to fit where I'm at in my life and what my quick-results goals are—whether it's a photo shoot or Victoria's Secret fashion show. He motivates me, and I also motivate myself, because my work's important to me—and let's face it, as a model, image is a huge part of it! Now, I have an additional reason, too. I really do want to be energized and healthy so I can keep up with my daughter as she gets a little older and starts running around. I think everyone should just come up with their own motivations for wanting to do the program and get in shape. Nothing really works if you're not committed to it for your own reasons.

My Journal

Use this space to write down how you feel emotionally and physically, what you eat, any challenges you are facing, and the time, duration, and intensity of your workout.

_____

_____

_____

_____

_____

_____

_____

_____

_____

_____

_____

_____

_____

_____

_____

_____

_____

_____

_____

Congratulations! You did it. You've completed the 14-day Ultimate New York Body Plan. I am proud of you! Please turn to Chapter 7 to find out how to maintain your results. The maintenance chapter will prove an invaluable tool that will be continually referred to. As I said at the outset, teaching you how to maintain your dramatic results is one of the things that is so often missing from other makeover programs. Mastering this skill will help you guarantee long-time success and a life-long transformation.

6
THE ULTIMATE RECIPE COLLECTION

In this chapter, you'll find recipes that make up the meal plans in Chapter 5. (Unless otherwise noted, each recipe is for one serving.) All the Ultimate New York Body Plan recipes follow my A, B, C, D, E, and F of nutrition. We worked hard not only to eliminate alcohol, bread, carbs, dairy products, extra sweets, and fruit, but also to design delicious meals. You will never feel deprived on this program. I've personally tested and tried each of these recipes—as have most of my clients. I'm confident that you will love them.

ULTIMATE BODY PLAN RECIPES

SCRAMBLED EGG WHITES WITH SHIITAKE MUSHROOMS AND TURKEY BACON

At the Madison Square Club, plain scrambled egg whites will never do. We've livened up this breakfast platter by adding sautéed shiitake mushrooms and turkey bacon.

2 strips turkey bacon

1 shiitake mushroom cap,
    cut into julienne strips

3 egg whites

1 tablespoon water

Freshly ground black pepper to taste

Garnish: $1/4$ teaspoon chopped
    fresh parsley

Heat a 9-inch nonstick skillet over medium heat and coat with nonfat, vegetable cooking spray.

Sauté the two strips of turkey bacon until cooked through and crispy—approximately 1 to 2 minutes for each side.

Remove the bacon and immediately place the mushroom strips into the same skillet and sauté until slightly browned—approximately 1 to 2 minutes. Remove from heat and set aside.

In a small bowl, whisk together the egg whites and water. Season to taste with pepper. Place the eggs in the nonstick skillet and stir until cooked through—approximately 1 minute or until the edges begin to set. Do not overcook.

Arrange the eggs and the mushrooms on a plate, sprinkle with parsley, and add the two strips of turkey bacon on the side.

SCRAMBLED EGG WHITES WITH GROUND TURKEY AND CHOPPED TOMATOES

This hearty, "stick to your ribs" meal is one of Linda Evangelista's favorites. It will fuel your morning in a low-fat, energetic way.

2 ounces ground turkey breast

Pinch ground coriander

Pinch salt and pepper

Pinch cayenne pepper

$1/4$ cup chopped fresh tomatoes

3 egg whites

1 tablespoon water

Heat a 9-inch nonstick skillet over medium heat and coat with nonfat vegetable cooking spray.

In a small bowl, mix the ground turkey breast with the coriander and cayenne pepper. Place in skillet and brown for about 1 minute.

Add the chopped tomatoes and continue to brown, stirring frequently. Cook for about 3 minutes or until cooked through. Remove turkey and tomatoes from pan and place skillet back on the fire.

In a small bowl, whisk together egg whites and water. Season to taste with salt and pepper.

Add the egg mixture to the skillet and cook for about 1 minute or until the edges begin to set.

Place the eggs, turkey, and tomatoes on a serving platter and serve immediately.

SPINACH AND BROCCOLI EGG WHITE FRITTATA

Created on the Isle of Capri, this Madison Square Club staple puts a little zip into an otherwise mundane breakfast. Try this with some turkey sausage or turkey bacon for an extra hearty meal.

3 egg whites
1 tablespoon water
Black pepper to taste

$1/4$ cup baby spinach leaves, washed and steamed
$1/4$ cup steamed broccoli florets

Option: Serve with turkey bacon or turkey sausage (2 strips or 2 links).

Preheat oven to 350°F.

In a medium-sized bowl, whisk together the egg whites and water. Season to taste with pepper. Pour into a 6-inch, round, ovenproof, baking dish.

Arrange the spinach and broccoli evenly over the egg mixture.

Bake for 15 to 20 minutes or until the center is just set. Do not overbake.

Let cool for 2 to 3 minutes. Serve immediately.

Roasted Red Pepper Frittata

With more vitamin C then oranges (and a whole lot fewer calories!), the addition of this vegetable really packs a powerful punch. I have given red peppers MVP (most valuable player status in my kitchen)

$^1/_4$ cup julienned, roasted,
    red bell pepper
1 teaspoon chopped fresh basil
3 egg whites

1 tablespoon water
Pinch cayenne pepper

Preheat oven to 350°F.

    Arrange peppers and basil in a 6-inch, ovenproof, baking dish.

    In a medium-sized bowl, whisk together egg whites and water. Season to taste with cayenne pepper. Pour over vegetable mixture.

    Bake for 15 to 20 minutes or until the center is just set.

Mushroom and Asparagus Frittata

A little added zip of mushrooms along with the natural diuretic properties of asparagus make this dish a real crowd-pleaser on this program.

2 teaspoons minced shallots
$^1/_4$ cup thinly sliced mushroom caps
1 teaspoon chopped fresh parsley
$^1/_4$ cup steamed, coarsely chopped
    asparagus

3 egg whites
1 tablespoon water
Freshly ground black pepper
    to taste

Preheat oven to 350°F.

    Heat a 6-inch, nonstick skillet over medium heat. Place the shallots and the mushroom caps in the skillet, add the chopped parsley, and brown for 2 minutes, stirring occasionally.

Place mushroom mixture into 6-inch, ovenproof, baking dish. Arrange cooked asparagus over mushroom mixture.

In a medium-sized bowl, whisk together eggs and water. Season with pepper. Pour egg mixture on top of vegetable mixture and bake for 15 to 20 minutes, until center is just set. Do not overbake.

DAVID'S ULTIMATE LOW-FAT EGG SALAD

This is the perfect to-go breakfast. When more time is available, serve on a bed of mesclun salad.

3 hard-boiled egg whites,
    coarsely chopped
$1/4$ cup chopped celery
1 teaspoon Dijon mustard

1 tablespoon chopped fresh parsley
1 slice cooked turkey bacon, coarsely
    chopped

In a small bowl, mix all ingredients.

SESAME CHICKEN FINGERS

This easy dish goes over well at parties. It's also great as a light meal when served with broccoli.

4 ounces boneless, skinless
    chicken breast sliced into
    4 strips
$1/4$ teaspoon low-sodium
    soy sauce

$1/4$ teaspoon Dijon mustard
1 teaspoon water
1 tablespoon turmeric
1 tablespoon toasted black and white
    sesame seeds

In a small bowl, marinate the chicken with the soy sauce, mustard, water, and turmeric up to 1 hour. Coat the chicken with sesame seeds.

Preheat oven to 350°F.

Place the chicken in a nonstick baking pan.

Bake for 12 to 15 minutes or until chicken strips are cooked through.

ALMOND CRUSTED CHICKEN

The almonds turn this otherwise ordinary chicken dish into a crunchy, nutritious meal that packs a healthy dose of vitamin E and fiber.

1 egg white

3 teaspoons water

Salt and pepper to taste

6 ounces boneless, skinless chicken breast, pounded thin

1/4 cup sliced almonds, coarsely chopped

Whisk egg white, water, salt, and pepper in small bowl. Dip the chicken breast into the egg mixture and dredge in almonds.

Heat a nonstick skillet over medium heat and lightly coat with nonfat vegetable spray.

Sauté chicken on one side over medium heat for 3 minutes. Turn and cook for an additional 3 to 4 minutes, until cooked through.

CHICKEN WITH RED PEPPER ALMOND PESTO

Who knew chicken had so many different disguises! The red pepper gives this dish a nice kick while providing lots of vitamin C.

6 ounces boneless, skinless chicken breast, pounded thin

2 tablespoons *Red Pepper Almond Pesto

1 teaspoon chopped fresh parsley

1 teaspoon chopped fresh basil

Preheat oven to 350°F.

Place chicken breast on an 8-inch aluminum foil square. Top chicken breast with Red Pepper Almond Pesto, parsley, and basil.

Roll chicken breast and wrap with aluminum foil. Place foil packet on an ovenproof dish or sheet.

Bake for 25 to 30 minutes or until cooked through.

CHICKEN MEATBALLS WITH TOMATO EGGPLANT SAUCE

You'll love this playful alternative to a Madison Square Club signature dish. The chicken lends itself nicely to this adaptation.

$^1/_4$ cup chopped Vidalia onion

1 teaspoon minced garlic

$^1/_2$ cup cubed eggplant

$^1/_2$ cup cubed zucchini

$^1/_2$ cup chopped roasted
    red peppers

2 plum tomatoes, chopped

$^1/_2$ cup chopped canned tomatoes

1 tablespoon fresh basil leaves,
    chopped fine

Freshly ground black pepper to taste

6 ounces ground chicken breast

1 egg white

1 teaspoon finely chopped shallots

1 teaspoon Dijon mustard

1 teaspoon chopped fresh basil

1 teaspoon chopped parsley

1 teaspoon chopped fresh mint

2 dashes hot pepper sauce

Heat a medium-sized, nonstick skillet over medium heat and lightly coat with nonfat vegetable cooking spray. Add the onions and garlic and cook for 2 to 3 minutes, until softened. Add the eggplant, zucchini, and roasted red peppers. Add the plum tomatoes, canned tomatoes, basil, and freshly ground pepper. Simmer gently for 15 minutes. Set aside.

In a medium-sized bowl, combine the chicken, egg white, shallots, mustard, basil, parsley, mint, black pepper, and hot pepper sauce. Mix gently and shape into two meatballs.

Heat a medium-sized, nonstick skillet over medium heat and coat with non-fat vegetable cooking spray. Add the meatballs and cook for 4 to 5 minutes, turning often until browned. Pour the tomato sauce over the meatballs in the skillet. Cover and simmer for 8 to 10 minutes, until the meatballs are cooked through.

Serving suggestion: Place chicken meatballs and tomato sauce on a bed of grilled julienned zucchini.

CHICKEN AND EGGPLANT WRAP

Good in the oven or on the grill, this versatile recipe is very easy to prepare.

$1/2$ small eggplant, sliced lengthwise $1/4$ inch thick, grilled or broiled until tender
Pinch salt

6 ounces boneless, skinless chicken breast, pounded thin
$1/8$ cup chopped tomato
1 teaspoon chopped fresh oregano
1 teaspoon chopped fresh basil

Spray a nonstick baking sheet with nonfat vegetable cooking spray. Place eggplant slices on the sheet, salt lightly, and broil until softened and charred—approximately 10 minutes. Set aside to cool.

Preheat oven to 350°F.

Place chicken breast on an 8-inch square of aluminum foil. Top with eggplant, chopped tomato, oregano, and basil.

Roll chicken breast and wrap with aluminum foil. Place on an ovenproof baking dish or baking sheet.

Bake for 30 minutes or until cooked through.

MEDITERRANEAN CHICKEN STIR-FRY

This good, healthy stir-fry is so delicious, you'll swear you're cheating on your nutrition plan.

6 ounces boneless, skinless
    chicken breast cut into
    1-inch strips
$1/2$ cup steamed cauliflower
    florets
$1/2$ teaspoon chopped fresh rosemary

1 teaspoon chopped fresh thyme
$1/8$ teaspoon freshly ground
    black pepper
$1/4$ cup chopped tomato
1 teaspoon chopped black olives

Heat a nonstick, 9-inch skillet over medium heat and coat with nonfat vegetable cooking spray.

Place chicken in skillet and sauté until brown, about 3 to 5 minutes.

Add cauliflower, herbs, and tomatoes and continue cooking for an additional 3 minutes.

Add olives and sauté for 1 minute.

MIDDLE EASTERN CHICKEN KABOB

A Middle Eastern rub makes this dish delectable and quite satisfying.

$1/2$ teaspoon ground cumin
$1/2$ teaspoon paprika
$1/4$ teaspoon coriander
$1/8$ teaspoon freshly ground
    black pepper

6 ounces boneless, skinless chicken
    breast cut in cubes
1 small zucchini, cubed
1 small onion, quartered

Combine the cumin, paprika, coriander, and freshly ground black pepper into a dry rub. Place the chicken cubes in a medium-sized mixing bowl and coat them with the dry rub. Cover the bowl and refrigerate for up to 3 hours.

Preheat oven to 350°F or prepare a grill.

Thread the chicken, cubed zucchini, and onions onto skewers and refrigerate until ready to cook.

Grill the kabobs, turning frequently, or broil in the oven for about 15 to 20 minutes or until cooked through.

ASIAN BBQ CHICKEN KABOB WITH THAI SALSA

A hint of the Far East turns plain chicken into a very impressive recipe that you will use over and over again.

1 teaspoon low-sodium
   soy sauce
$^1/_4$ teaspoon wasabi powder
   or hot chili paste
$^1/_2$ teaspoon grated fresh ginger
6 ounces boneless, skinless
   chicken breast cut into
   4 long strips

$^1/_2$ cup chopped fresh mint
$^1/_4$ teaspoon seeded and
   chopped jalapeño peppers
2 tablespoons chopped fresh
   cilantro
2 teaspoons white wine vinegar
$^1/_2$ cup chopped cucumber

In a medium-sized mixing bowl, combine $^1/_2$ teaspoon of the soy sauce, wasabi powder, and fresh ginger and mix well.

Place the chicken in the bowl and coat well. Thread the chicken strips on skewers and refrigerate for up to 3 hours.

In a medium-sized mixing bowl, combine the mint, jalapeño peppers, the other $^1/_2$ teaspoon soy sauce, cilantro, vinegar, and cucumber and stir well. Cover with plastic wrap and refrigerate until ready to use.

Prepare grill or preheat oven to 350°F.

Bake or grill for 15 to 20 minutes or until cooked through.

Serving suggestion: Serve chicken with *Spicy Thai Salsa and sautéed spinach and shiitake mushrooms.

Jamaican Jerk Chicken

Back to the islands, "mon." This chicken will have you craving to go. The only no-no, of course, would be the Jamaican rum.

$1/2$ teaspoon ground allspice

$1/2$ teaspoon dried thyme

$3/4$ teaspoon cayenne pepper

$3/4$ teaspoon freshly ground
   black pepper

$3/4$ teaspoon ground sage

$1/4$ teaspoon ground nutmeg

$1/4$ teaspoon ground cinnamon

$1/2$ teaspoon minced garlic

$1/8$ cup low-sodium soy sauce

$1/4$ cup white vinegar

1 small jalapeño pepper, seeded and
   diced

1 scallion, chopped fine

1 small onion, chopped fine

6 ounces boneless, skinless chicken
   breast

In a medium-sized bowl combine the allspice, thyme, cayenne pepper, black pepper, sage, nutmeg, cinnamon, and garlic. With a wire whisk, slowly add the soy sauce and vinegar. Add the jalapeño pepper, scallion, and small onion and mix well.

Marinate the chicken breast in the mixture for 1 to 2 hours.

Remove the breasts from the marinade and grill for 6 minutes on each side or until fully cooked. Baste with the marinade.

Chicken and Shiitake Mushroom Burger

This is a real staple in the Ultimate New York Body Plan because its versatility allows it to be used as an entrée with spinach or broccoli or as a midafternoon snack.

4 ounces ground chicken breast

$1/4$ teaspoon Cajun seasoning

$1/4$ teaspoon Worcestershire
   sauce

1 tablespoon chopped onion

2 small shiitake mushrooms,
   chopped

In a medium-sized mixing bowl, combine the ground chicken with the Cajun seasoning and the Worcestershire sauce. Set aside.

Heat a skillet over medium heat and coat with nonfat vegetable cooking spray. Place the onion in the skillet and sauté until soft—approximately 1 to 2 minutes. Add the mushrooms and sauté for an additional 1 to 2 minutes. Remove skillet from heat and set aside.

Mix onion-mushroom mixture into ground chicken breast. Form this mixture into a burger. Sauté over medium heat for 3 minutes per side or until cooked through.

BARE BONES LOW-FAT
CHICKEN SALAD

One of the Madison Square Club MVPs, this chicken salad is versatile and quick and easy to prepare.

4 ounces poached chicken breast, cut into 1-inch cubes.

$^1/_4$ cup coarsely chopped celery

1 teaspoon finely chopped parsley

1 tablespoon sliced almonds, coarsely chopped

2 teaspoons Dijon mustard

2 tablespoons chicken stock

1 or 2 dashes hot pepper sauce

Salt and pepper to taste

In a medium-sized bowl, mix chicken, celery, parsley, and almonds.

In another bowl, whisk Dijon mustard, chicken stock, and hot pepper sauce together until well blended.

Add mustard mixture to chicken and mix well. Add salt and pepper to taste.

BASQUE STYLE CHICKEN

Anything but ordinary, this chicken packs a lot of flavor yet stays low in fat and carbs.

$1/4$ cup chopped onion
$1/2$ cup diced red bell pepper
$1/4$ teaspoon dried marjoram
$1/8$ teaspoon freshly ground
    black pepper
Pinch cayenne pepper
Pinch salt

1 strip cooked turkey bacon,
    coarsely chopped
$1/2$ cup chopped canned tomatoes
2 tablespoons water
6 ounces boneless, skinless
    chicken breast
1 teaspoon chopped fresh parsley

Preheat oven to 350°F.

Place a medium-sized, nonstick, ovenproof skillet over medium heat and coat with nonfat vegetable cooking spray. Add the onions, red pepper, marjoram, black pepper, cayenne pepper, and salt and sauté until soft—approximately 3 minutes. Add the turkey bacon, tomatoes, and water and stir.

Place chicken over vegetable mixture, cover, and bake for about 40 minutes or until chicken is cooked through.

Top with chopped fresh parsley.

Serving suggestion: Serve with grilled asparagus.

TURKEY LASAGNA

I know what you're thinking, "Isn't pasta a no-no?" That will never do at the Madison Square Club. Try this and you'll never place another penne in your mouth! Either as a snack or for lunch with a nice tossed green salad, this is quite a dish!

$1/2$ small eggplant, cut lengthwise
    in $1/4$-inch slices

Pinch freshly ground black pepper
Pinch cayenne pepper

$^{1}/_{2}$ small zucchini, cut lengthwise in $^{1}/_{4}$-inch slices

4 ounces ground turkey breast

$^{1}/_{4}$ teaspoon ground coriander

$^{1}/_{2}$ cup *Marinara Sauce

1 teaspoon chopped fresh basil

Preheat oven to 400°F.

Lightly coat a nonstick cookie sheet with nonfat vegetable cooking spray. Place eggplant and zucchini slices on the sheet, cover with foil, and bake for about 15 minutes or until slices are soft. Remove from oven and set aside.

Heat a skillet over medium heat and coat with nonfat vegetable cooking spray. Place ground turkey, coriander, black pepper, and cayenne pepper in the skillet and sauté until brown—approximately 3 to 4 minutes.

Lasagna assembly: Lightly spray an ovenproof baking dish with nonfat vegetable cooking spray. Alternate layers of baked eggplant, ground turkey, marinara sauce, and baked zucchini. Top with marinara sauce. Repeat the process if necessary.

Bake for 15 minutes or until heated through.

Top with chopped fresh basil.

TURKEY CHILI

The all-time favorite at the Madison Square Club is brought back here by popular demand. Here, I've gotten a little stricter and eliminated the carrots that were added in Sound Mind, Sound Body. *I promise you won't miss them, and in their place, I've added vitamin C rich red pepper.*

1 pound lean ground turkey

1 cup red pepper, coarsely chopped

1 onion, coarsely chopped ($^{3}/_{4}$ cup)

1 teaspoon paprika

1 teaspoon ground cumin

$^{1}/_{8}$ teaspoon ground cayenne pepper

1 can (14 $^{1}/_{2}$ ounces) chopped plum tomatoes in juice

2/3 rib celery, coarsely chopped
   (2/3 cup)
1 clove garlic, minced
2 teaspoons chili powder

1/2 cup chicken stock or low-fat, low-sodium chicken broth
1 bay leaf
Salt and pepper to taste

Heat a 3-quart, nonstick saucepan over high heat and coat with cooking spray. Add the turkey and season to taste with the salt and pepper. Cook for 2 to 3 minutes, breaking up the turkey into pieces, until browned all over. Remove to a bowl, and cover with foil to keep warm.

Reduce the heat to low, and add the peppers, onion, celery, and garlic. Cook for 3 to 5 minutes, until the vegetables begin to soften. Add the chili powder, paprika, cumin, and cayenne pepper. Cook, stirring, for 1 minute. Increase the heat to medium, and add the tomatoes, stock, and bay leaf. Bring to a boil over high heat. Reduce the heat to medium-low and simmer for 15 minutes, uncovered.

Add the browned turkey, and simmer for 5 minutes more. Remove and discard the bay leaf before serving.

Makes 4 servings.

TURKEY AND SPINACH BURGER

Serve this healthy alternative to the McDonald's burger with ratatouille and you have a delicious and yes, nutritious, satisfying meal.

6 ounces no-fat ground
   turkey breast
1/2 cup chopped spinach,
   sautéed and drained

1/8 teaspoon salt
1/8 teaspoon black pepper
Pinch grated nutmeg

Combine ingredients and form into a burger. Grill or broil burger 4 minutes on each side or until cooked through.

Serving suggestion: Use one tablespoon of *Red Pepper Almond Pesto instead of ketchup to add some zip to your burger.

STUFFED RED PEPPER WITH GROUND TURKEY

This dish always reminds me of Sunday meals at my mom's house. Whatever your memories, this is a sure winner.

6 ounces ground turkey breast
1 scallion, thinly sliced
1/4 teaspoon dried oregano
1/4 teaspoon dried thyme

1 teaspoon fresh chopped parsley
Pinch salt and pepper
1 red bell pepper with top cut off,
    seeded and hollowed

Preheat oven to 400°F.

In a medium-sized mixing bowl, combine turkey, scallion, oregano, and thyme.

Heat a nonstick skillet and coat with nonfat vegetable cooking spray. Place turkey mixture in skillet and brown for 2–3 minutes. Remove from heat and add parsley, salt, and pepper.

Fill the red pepper with the ground turkey mixture and place into a baking dish. Place 2 tablespoons of water into the baking dish and cover with foil. Bake for 15 minutes, then remove foil and bake an additional 5 minutes.

Optional variation: Before baking, place one tablespoon of *Marinara Sauce on top of the ground turkey.

MEXICAN TURKEY BURGER
WITH JALAPEÑO PEPPERS AND MEXICAN SALSA

My favorite ethnic food has got to be Mexican—can never really get enough salsa! Mix the all-American burger, give it a little South of the Border flavor, and you've got this fresh and zippy dish. The salsa can also be used for your egg dishes and anything else that might need to be a little caliente.

Mexican Salsa
1/2 cup chopped tomatoes
1 tablespoon scallion chopped
    (white part only)

1/2 tablespoon fresh cilantro
1 teaspoon white wine vinegar

Turkey Burger

What can I say about turkey burgers other than I'd be lost without them! Just remember, there are no buns in this recipe!

4 ounces ground turkey breast

1 tablespoon chopped scallion
  (white part only)

1/2 teaspoon jalapeño pepper,
  seeded and minced

1/2 teaspoon minced garlic

3/4 teaspoon chili powder

1/4 teaspoon ground cumin

Pinch of salt

In a medium-sized bowl, combine the tomatoes, scallion, cilantro, and white wine vinegar. Mix well, cover, and refrigerate. This can be made ahead of time and keeps well for 2 to 3 days.

In another medium-sized bowl, combine turkey, scallion, jalapeño pepper, garlic, chili powder, cumin, and salt and mix thoroughly. Shape mixture into patty.

Grill turkey burger for 4 to 5 minutes on each side until cooked through.

Top with the Mexican Salsa.

SALMON CAKE

Heart-healthy salmon is adaptable and quite tasty, as you will see in this recipe.

1 egg white

4 ounces wild salmon fillet, ground

1 teaspoon chopped fresh parsley

1 teaspoon white wine vinegar

1/2 teaspoon Worcestershire sauce

1/4 teaspoon red pepper flakes

In a large bowl, beat egg white until thick. In another bowl, combine salmon, parsley, vinegar, Worcestershire sauce, and red pepper flakes. Carefully fold egg white into salmon mixture.

Heat a medium-sized, nonstick skillet over medium heat and coat with nonfat vegetable cooking spray.

Spoon mixture onto the skillet, forming salmon cake about 4 inches wide and 1 inch thick.

Cook over medium heat for 3 minutes and then turn over and cook for an additional 2 minutes for medium rare.

FENNEL CRUSTED SALMON

The distinctive flavor of fennel transforms this dish.

1 cup baby arugula, washed
    and drained well
$1/4$ fennel bulb, cut into very
    thin strips
$1/4$ cup roasted red bell
    pepper strips

$1/2$ tablespoon chopped basil leaves
1 teaspoon fennel seed
1 teaspoon black peppercorns
1 wild salmon fillet, about 4 ounces
Pinch salt

Preheat oven to 400°F.

In a medium-sized bowl combine the arugula, fennel, pepper strips, basil, and vinegar; toss well.

Crush the fennel seed and the peppercorns using a mortar and pestle or a spice grinder. Season the top of the salmon fillet with the salt and sprinkle the fennel-pepper mix over the fillet. Press the seasoning into the flesh with your fingertips.

Heat a large nonstick, ovenproof, sauté pan over medium heat and coat with nonfat vegetable cooking spray. Place the salmon fillet spice side down into the skillet and sear until the fillet edges have begun to crisp slightly, about 3 minutes.

Transfer the pan into the oven and bake 3 to 5 minutes (until desired doneness).

Arrange arugula, fennel bulb, red pepper, and basil onto plate and top with salmon.

SPICY WASABI SALMON BURGER

This is one of my favorite burgers! It's great as a lunch served with spinach or as an afternoon snack.

1 teaspoon wasabi powder

1 teaspoon water

$1/2$ teaspoon Dijon mustard

4 ounces wild salmon fillet,
    cut into $1/2$-inch cubes

1 egg white, lightly beaten

$1/2$ tablespoon low-sodium soy sauce

1 teaspoon black sesame seeds

In a medium-sized bowl mix water with wasabi powder and whisk until blended.

Add Dijon mustard, salmon, egg white, soy sauce, and sesame seeds and stir until mixed well.

Form into burger and grill 2 to 3 minutes per side (or until desired doneness).

ASIAN STYLE SALMON

The addition of ginger makes this dish delicious, nutritious, and tasty! It is good served hot or at room temperature.

$3/4$ teaspoon low-sodium
    soy sauce

1 teaspoon wasabi powder

$1/2$ teaspoon grated fresh ginger

6-ounce wild salmon steak

1 scallion, thinly sliced (white part only)

In a medium-sized mixing bowl, combine the soy sauce, wasabi, and ginger. Marinate the salmon with the soy sauce mixture in a shallow baking dish for 30 minutes at room temperature or for 2 to 3 hours in the refrigerator.

Place on grill and cook for 2 to 3 minutes on each side for medium rare.

Place salmon on top of vegetables (see below) and garnish with thinly sliced scallions.

Serving suggestion: Serve with *Bok Choy with Red Peppers and Almonds.

SALMON
FLORENTINE

When joining two nutrition MVPs—salmon and spinach—how can you go wrong?

6 ounces center cut salmon steak

Freshly ground black pepper

1 cup packed fresh baby spinach
    leaves

$^1/_4$ cup *Marinara Sauce

1 tablespoon *Red Pepper Almond
    Pesto

Preheat oven to 400°F.

Season the salmon with pepper.

Heat an ovenproof sauté pan and spray with vegetable oil spray. Sear salmon 1–2 minutes per side. Remove pan from heat.

Top the salmon with fresh spinach, Red Pepper Almond Pesto, and Marinara Sauce.

Bake for 8 to10 minutes or until spinach is wilted.

TUNA AND SHRIMP KABOB

This is a really fun party dish and can easily be adapted to serve more people.

$^1/_2$ small eggplant

$^1/_2$ medium-sized, yellow bell pepper

4 ounces skinless tuna steak,
    cut into four 1-inch cubes

2 medium shrimp, peeled and cleaned

$^1/_3$ cup water

1 teaspoon Dijon mustard

1 teaspoon chopped fresh dill

Preheat oven to 400°F.

Cut eggplant in half lengthwise, then cut diagonally into 1/2-inch pieces; set aside. Cut pepper into quarters; remove seeds and stem. Cut each piece in half. Bake peppers and eggplant in foil packet for 20 minutes. Remove and cool.

Place peppers and eggplant on skewers. Place tuna and shrimp on skewers, alternating tuna then shrimp. Place all skewers in a large shallow dish.

Combine water, Dijon mustard, and dill in a small bowl. Mix well and pour over kabobs. Cover and refrigerate 30 minutes. Remove kabobs from marinade; discard marinade.

Spray grill rack with nonfat vegetable cooking spray. Place kabobs on grill.

Grill tuna/shrimp skewers 2 to 3 minutes each side and veggies 4 minutes on each side.

SEARED TUNA BURGER

Burgers come in so many different styles—this is one of the healthy ones.

1 tablespoon finely chopped
    shallots

6 ounces tuna steak, cut into
    $^1/_2$-inch cubes

1 teaspoon chopped fresh
   parsley

1 teaspoon Dijon mustard

$1/4$ cup grated daikon radish

1 lightly beaten egg white

Salt and pepper to taste

In a medium-sized bowl, combine all ingredients until well blended. Form into a burger.

Grill 2 to 3 minutes on each side (or until desired doneness).

TUNA COBB
SALAD

This is my version of Cobb salad for all of you who don't eat turkey or are just in the mood to tweak an old standby.

2 cups mesclun salad

2 spears cooked asparagus,
   chopped coarsely

$1/2$ cup seeded and chopped tomato

1 hard-boiled egg white,
   chopped coarsely

1 strip (2 ounces) turkey bacon,
   cooked and crumbled

4 ounces tuna steak

Salt and pepper to taste

Red wine vinegar to taste

In a large salad bowl, arrange mesclun salad, asparagus, tomato, egg, and bacon.

Season tuna steak with salt and pepper.

Heat a nonstick skillet over medium heat and coat with nonfat vegetable oil spray. Sear tuna 2 to 3 minutes on each side. Remove tuna from pan and place on salad.

Drizzle with 1 or 2 tablespoons of red wine vinegar.

Striped Bass with
Mint Parsley Pesto

I tried a version of this while on the Mediterranean at a restaurant in Positano. Try this dish, and imagine you too are on the Amalfi coast.

1 4-ounce striped bass fillet
$1/4$ cup mint leaves
2 tablespoons parsley leaves
$1/4$ teaspoon salt

$1/4$ teaspoon freshly ground black pepper
2 tablespoons water
$1/2$ teaspoon olive oil

Blend mint, parsley, salt, pepper, water, and oil in a miniblender.

Place the fish in a small dish, coat it with the blend, and let sit in the dish for 15 minutes.

Grill 2 to 3 minutes per side or until cooked through.

Curried Almond
Striped Bass

Remember what I said about the importance of flavor, herbs, and crunch. You'll find the combination of the almonds and the curry scintillating and, at the same time, healthy.

$1/8$ cup chopped raw almonds
$1/8$ teaspoon salt
$1/8$ teaspoon freshly ground black pepper

Pinch cayenne pepper
$1/4$ teaspoon curry powder
4 ounces striped bass fillet

In a small mixing bowl, mix all the ingredients except the bass fillet.

Lightly coat the fillet with nonfat vegetable cooking spray. Rub one side of the fillet with the almond and herb mixture until well coated.

Heat a nonstick, sauté pan over medium heat and coat with nonfat vegetable cooking spray. Place fillet in pan almond side down and cook for 2 to 3 minutes. Turn fillet over and cook an additional 2 minutes.

Serving suggestion: Serve alongside sautéed julienne of zucchini and red pepper strips.

SHRIMP ON CABBAGE BED WITH MUSTARD DRESSING SALAD

You'll love this quick and easy dish!

4 ounces cleaned, cooked, and
    peeled shrimp, chopped
    coarsely and chilled
$^3/_4$ cup shredded green cabbage
$^3/_4$ cup shredded red cabbage
$^1/_2$ cup chopped tomato
$^1/_2$ cup red bell pepper strips
$^1/_4$ cup chopped green bell
    pepper

$^1/_2$ cup sliced Kirby cucumber
    (with skin)
$^1/_4$ cup daikon radish, julienned
1 teaspoon olive oil
3 teaspoons white wine vinegar
$^1/_2$ teaspoon Dijon mustard
Pinch salt
Pinch freshly ground black pepper
1 teaspoon finely chopped dill

In a large mixing bowl, combine the shrimp, cabbage, tomato, red and green pepper, cucumber, and radish.

In a small bowl, whisk the oil, vinegar, mustard, salt, and pepper.

Pour dressing over salad.

Garnish with dill, and serve.

MUSTARD CRUSTED HALIBUT

The addition of whole grain mustard (the most indispensable accompaniment in my kitchen) and lots of fresh herbs makes this fish dish seem more exotic then dietetic. Don't be bashful when adding the whole grain mustard. In this case, if some is good, a little more won't do any harm!

6 ounces center cut halibut steak

1 teaspoon whole grain mustard

1 teaspoon chopped fresh thyme

1 tablespoon chopped fresh oregano

1 teaspoon chopped fresh rosemary

$1/2$ teaspoon freshly ground black pepper

1 teaspoon water

Preheat oven to 350°F.

In a small bowl, combine the mustard, thyme, oregano, rosemary, pepper, and water and blend well. The mixture should be pastelike.

Place halibut in an ovenproof baking dish and spread mustard-herb mixture on the fish. Bake halibut for 15 to 20 minutes, or until fish is flaky.

Serving suggestion: Serve on a bed of baby spinach, arugula, and water chestnuts.

FLOUNDER WITH ARUGULA ALMOND PESTO

Who knew pesto could be so healthy? The Arugula Almond Pesto definitely makes this potentially mundane meal a real winner.

6 ounces flounder fillet

2 tablespoons *Arugula Almond Pesto

Preheat oven to 350°F.

Spray an ovenproof dish with vegetable spray. Place flounder in dish and cover with pesto. Bake for 15 minutes or until flounder is flaky.

DAVID'S
PANTRY AND SIDE DISHES

Before you start the program, stock up on the following assortment of side dishes and pantry items. It will reduce your preparation time in the kitchen during the next 14 days, making the program go more smoothly.

VEGETABLE SOUP

What healthy kitchen would be complete without this hearty, low-carb soup? Serve as a meal with a salmon burger or as a snack.

1 teaspoon whole black
   peppercorns
1 bay leaf
1 teaspoon fresh oregano
$1/2$-inch slice fresh ginger
5–8 sprigs fresh parsley
1 small zucchini, thinly sliced
1 red bell pepper, seeded and
   chopped coarsely

1 small onion, chopped
2 shiitake mushrooms, sliced
1 celery stalk, chopped coarsely
$1/2$ teaspoon salt
4 cups water
$1/2$ cup chopped tomato

Place peppercorns, bay leaf, oregano, ginger, and parsley in cheesecloth.

Place the zucchini, red pepper, onion, mushrooms, celery, salt, peppercorn and bay leaf pouch, and water in a 2-quart saucepan. Bring to a boil, then reduce heat to low-medium and let it simmer, skimming off the foam.

Let cook for 45 minutes to 1 hour.

In the last 5 minutes of cooking, add chopped tomato. When cooking is done, remove bay leaf and peppercorn pouch.

Makes 4 servings.

Tomato Soup

The only thing missing from the soup and sandwich combo of your youth will be the sandwich. Few things are more satisfying and comforting on a chilly Sunday afternoon than tomato soup.

1 large Vidalia onion, chopped
1 zucchini, chopped
1 teaspoon chopped fresh thyme
6 large tomatoes, skinned, seeded,
    and chopped

2 cups fat-free chicken broth
1 tablespoon chopped dill
Garnish: 2 scallions, thinly sliced

Heat a medium-sized saucepan and spray with nonfat vegetable cooking spray. Cook onion, zucchini, and thyme over medium heat until soft and beginning to lightly brown—about 8 minutes.

Add the tomatoes and chicken broth and bring to a boil. Reduce heat and continue to simmer for about 20 minutes.

Stir in the chopped dill and continue to simmer for an additional 10 minutes.

To serve, garnish with thinly sliced scallions.

Makes 4 servings.

Spinach and Shiitake Mushroom Stir-Fry

This healthy and versatile side dish can be used throughout the day. This dish would've stopped Popeye in his tracks.

1 teaspoon minced shallots
$^1/_2$ teaspoon minced garlic
1 shiitake mushroom, thinly sliced
1 cup spinach leaves, washed and
    dried well

1 teaspoon low-sodium
    soy sauce
1 tablespoon minced, peeled, fresh
    ginger

Heat a nonstick sauté pan on high heat and spray with cooking spray. Add shallots and garlic and sauté until soft, 1 to 2 minutes. Add shiitake mushroom slices and sauté until all ingredients are lightly browned. Set aside.

Place spinach, soy sauce, and ginger in the pan and sauté until spinach is wilted. Add the mushroom mixture, stir, and continue to cook for an additional minute. Serve as a side dish.

PUREED BROCCOLI AND ROASTED RED PEPPERS

This tastes great as a solo act as a snack or in a supporting role as a side dish. The broccoli packs lots of calcium, and the red peppers lots of vitamin C.

1 cup cooked broccoli florets
1 tablespoon roasted red peppers
1 tablespoon chicken stock

Combine all the ingredients in a food processor. Pulse until well blended.

BOK CHOY WITH RED PEPPERS AND ALMONDS

Between the vitamin C rich red pepper and the vitamin E dense almonds, this dish is what "delicious and nutritious" is all about.

2 tablespoons blanched
   sliced almonds
1 cup sliced bok choy

$^1/_2$ cup sliced red bell peppers
Salt and pepper to taste

Spray nonstick sauté pan with vegetable cooking spray and heat pan. Add almonds and sauté until lightly browned, about 1 to 2 minutes.

Add red pepper and bok choy and continue to sauté until vegetables begin to soften (3 minutes).

Season to taste with salt and pepper.

RATATOUILLE

As a side dish or a snack, this dish can be made and used for several days. OK, so the French baguette won't do.

6 Italian plum tomatoes, diced
    into 1-inch cubes
12 ounces canned crushed
    tomatoes
1 tablespoon minced fresh oregano
$^1/_4$ teaspoon freshly ground black
    pepper
1 pound eggplant, diced into
    $^1/_2$-inch cubes, salted, and
    drained

1 pound yellow squash, diced into
    1-inch cubes
1 pound zucchini, diced into 1-inch
    cubes
$^1/_2$ pound yellow onion, diced into
    1-inch cubes
$^1/_2$ pound red bell pepper, diced into
    1-inch cubes
1 tablespoon organic extra-virgin
    olive oil
1 ounce small capers, drained

Preheat oven to 400°F.

In a medium-sized mixing bowl, combine tomatoes, crushed tomatoes, oregano, and black pepper; set aside.

In a medium-sized roasting pan, combine eggplant, squash, zucchini, onion, and bell pepper, coat with olive oil, and cover with foil. Bake 45 minutes; stir once during cooking.

Stir in tomato mixture and bake an additional 20 minutes, uncovered. Stir in capers.

Serving suggestions: Ratatouille is the perfect side dish with grilled fresh turkey breast, Salmon Florentine, or Chicken and Shiitake Mushroom Burger.

Serves 4 to 6 people.

RED PEPPER ALMOND PESTO

What's in a name? By adding the red pepper and the almonds and losing the cheese and the oil, we've made an otherwise tasty but fattening dish a healthy and versatile staple in your newly transformed healthy kitchen.

2 red bell peppers, cored, seeded, and quartered
1 shallot, peeled

$1/4$ cup roasted blanched almonds
1 large garlic clove, smashed
Pinch salt and pepper

Place the peppers, shallots, almonds, and garlic in a blender or food processor. Salt and pepper to taste. Blend until finely minced.

Makes $1\,1/2$ cups.

Serving size: 1 tablespoon.

ARUGULA ALMOND PESTO

Yet another healthy variety to replace the fat-laden pesto of your past. The peppery taste of the arugula complements the almonds for a unique flavor combination.

1 $1/3$ cups packed fresh arugula leaves
$1/3$ cup packed fresh flat leaf parsley leaves
$1/2$ cup packed spinach leaves

2 tablespoons blanched almonds, toasted
1 large garlic clove, smashed
1 tablespoon extra-virgin olive oil
Pinch of salt and pepper

Place the arugula, parsley, spinach, almonds, and garlic in a blender or food processor. Process until finely minced. Add the oil and process until blended.

Season with salt and pepper to taste.

Makes about 3/4 cup.

COLESLAW VINAIGRETTE

Make sure to have plenty of this crowd favorite on hand.

2 cups thinly shredded green
    cabbage
$1/_4$ cup thinly sliced scallion
1 teaspoon caraway seeds
1 cup shredded red and yellow
    bell peppers

1 teaspoon low-sodium soy sauce
1 teaspoon toasted sesame seeds
2 teaspoons grated peeled ginger
1 tablespoon rice wine vinegar
Salt and pepper to taste

In a medium-sized bowl, combine all ingredients and mix well. May be made ahead of time and refrigerated.

CHICKEN STOCK

As fat intake is limited on this nutrition plan, chicken stock will take the place of things like mayonnaise, cream, and other sauces that you may use in your foods. Make sure to have plenty on hand; it freezes well.

1 whole chicken (3 pounds)
4 quarts cold bottled water
1 Vidalia onion, chopped
2 celery ribs, greens included,
    chopped

2 scallions, chopped
3 parsley sprigs
3 dill sprigs
1 tablespoon tricolor peppercorns
1 bay leaf

Wash and cut the chicken into pieces at the joints (or have your butcher do it). Place the chicken in a large stockpot. Add the water and bring to a boil over high heat. Skim any foam that rises to the surface.

Add the Vidalia onion, celery, and scallions. Return to a boil, then immediately reduce the heat to medium-low. Gently simmer for 2 hours, uncovered, skimming the foam occasionally and adding more water if necessary to keep the chicken submerged.

Wrap the parsley, dill, peppercorns, and bay leaf in cheesecloth and add to liquid. Simmer for 1 hour more.

Strain the stock through a sieve, pressing the solids to extract the liquid. Discard the solids. Pull the chicken off of the bones and reserve for another use. Let the stock cool to room temperature, then refrigerate until cold. Remove and discard fat as it congeals on surface. Pour the stock into ice cube trays and freeze until solid. Transfer the cubes to freezer bags and freeze for up to 3 months.

ROASTED RED PEPPERS

Red peppers actually have more vitamin C than oranges—and far fewer calories too!

3 red bell peppers

Preheat the broiler.

Cut off the tops of the peppers. Remove the core and seeds from each. Cut the peppers lengthwise into quarters. Lay the pieces skin side up on a baking pan.

Broil until the skin is charred. Remove from the heat.

Place the peppers in a small brown paper bag and fold the bag down.

When the peppers are cool enough to handle, remove and discard the skin using a paring knife. The skins should come off pretty easily.

Use immediately or freeze in an airtight plastic bag for up to 3 weeks.

MARINARA SAUCE

This sauce is the most versatile and popular of all of my club's sauces. Whether for fish, meat, or poultry, it definitely makes its presence felt.

1 Vidalia onion, chopped

6 plum tomatoes, chopped

1 cup chopped canned tomatoes

$1/2$ cup fresh basil leaves, finely chopped

Heat a medium-sized, nonstick skillet over medium heat and coat with cooking spray. Add the onion and cook for 2–3 minutes, until softened. Add the plum tomatoes, canned tomatoes, and basil. Simmer gently for 15 minutes. Let it cool and refrigerate for 3 to 5 days, or place in freezer until ready to use.

Serving size: 1 to 2 tablespoons per portion of fish or chicken should definitely do the trick.

ULTIMATE MAINTENANCE RECIPES

The following assortment of recipes, while delicious, each contains little cheats that make them unacceptable for your two-week plan, but perfect for your maintenance diet.

V8 SALAD DRESSING

No wonder the ad goes, "I should've had a V8!" What a delicious and refreshing way to dress an otherwise naked and boring salad.

5.5 ounces low-sodium V8

1 teaspoon balsamic vinegar

1 teaspoon oregano

$1/8$ teaspoon cayenne pepper

1 tablespoon chopped shallots

¹/₄ teaspoon thyme

¹/₈ teaspoon freshly ground
    black pepper

1 teaspoon Dijon mustard

Pinch cayenne pepper

In a small bowl, combine all the ingredients and mix well. Place in refrigerator and chill until ready to use.

    Shake before using.

MEDITERRANEAN SALSA WITH OLIVES

You'll love this condiment atop your turkey or spinach burger.

¹/₄ cup finely chopped, fresh,
    flat leaf parsley

1 teaspoon chopped black olives

¹/₄ cup chopped roasted red bell
    pepper

1 tablespoon cooked white beans

1 dash hot sauce

Freshly ground black pepper to taste

1 teaspoon chopped fresh parsley

In a medium-sized bowl, combine all the ingredients and mix well. Refrigerate until ready to use.

SPICY THAI SALSA

The mint and the fresh lime juice make this a perfect accompaniment to any seafood dish. As is the case with all my salsa dishes, a little goes a long way.

¹/₄ cup chopped mint

¹/₄ teaspoon chopped jalapeño
    peppers, seeded and chopped

¹/₂ teaspoon lime juice

¹/₄ cup fresh cilantro, chopped

In a small bowl, combine all the ingredients and blend well. This can be made ahead of time and refrigerated for up to 2 to 3 days.

Hawaiian Halibut with Spicy Salsa

The papaya really works well with the jalapeño pepper in this recipe, giving the halibut a nice little kick.

6 ounces center cut halibut
   steak
Pinch salt
Pinch freshly ground black
   pepper
$1/4$ cup chopped papaya
$1/4$ cup chopped red pepper

$1/4$ cup chopped yellow bell pepper
$1/4$ teaspoon jalapeño pepper,
   seeded and chopped
$1/8$ teaspoon grated fresh ginger
1 teaspoon lime juice
Pinch freshly ground black pepper

Season halibut with salt and pepper.

In a medium-sized bowl, combine the papaya, red and yellow pepper, jalapeño pepper, ginger, and lime juice. Mix well and season with black pepper. (This can be made ahead time and refrigerated for 2 to 3 days.)

Place halibut on hot grill for approximately 3 to 4 minutes per side, or until cooked through.

Top with salsa and serve immediately.

Low-Fat Chicken Salad with Yogurt and Green Apples

Similar to the original chicken salad recipe in your two-week plan, this recipe substitutes one tablespoon of plain fat-free yogurt for one of the tablespoons of chicken stock. It also includes some green apples.

4 ounces chicken breast, broiled
   and cut into 1-inch cubes,
$1/4$ cup coarsely chopped celery
$1/4$ cup chopped green apples

2 teaspoons Dijon mustard
1 tablespoon chicken stock
1 tablespoon no-fat plain yogurt
Freshly ground black pepper

1 tablespoon sliced blanched
   almonds, chopped coarsely

1 teaspoon finely chopped
   parsley

In a medium-sized bowl, combine chicken, celery, parsley, apples, and almonds.

In another bowl, whisk Dijon mustard, chicken stock, and no-fat plain yogurt until well blended.

Pour mustard mixture over chicken and mix together well. Add pepper to taste.

CITRUS AND FENNEL CRUSTED SALMON

Similar to a salmon recipe in your two-week plan, in this recipe we've added a little citrus—orange and lemon juice—and substituted balsamic vinegar for the wine vinegar. You've worked hard over the last two weeks, so treat yourself a little.

1 tablespoon fennel seed

1 tablespoon black peppercorns

1 salmon fillet, about 4 ounces

1 cup baby arugula, washed and
   drained well

$1/4$ fennel bulb, cut into very
   thin strips

$1/4$ cup roasted red bell pepper,
   cut into strips

1 teaspoon extra-virgin olive oil

$1/2$ tablespoon chopped basil leaves

1 teaspoon fresh lemon juice

1 tablespoon freshly squeezed orange
   juice

1 teaspoon balsamic vinegar

Follow the recipe for *Fennel Crusted Salmon and just add the lemon juice, orange juice, and balsamic vinegar to dress the baby arugula.

Citrus Ginger Striped Bass

Citrus and ginger will definitely make this a light, refreshing, crowd-pleaser.

$1/_4$ tablespoon finely shredded
orange peel
$1/_8$ cup freshly squeezed orange
juice
$1/_8$ cup lime juice

$3/_4$ teaspoon shredded ginger
1 tablespoon white wine vinegar
$3/_4$ teaspoon chopped cilantro
6 ounces striped bass

In a medium-sized bowl, combine all the ingredients and blend well.

Place the bass in a baking dish, cover, and marinate for 30 minutes to 1 hour.

Place on grill and cook for 2 to 3 minutes per side or until cooked through.

Shrimp Rolled in Lettuce

This is one of my favorite maintenance meals!

2 tablespoons lemon juice
1 teaspoon lemon zest
$1/_2$ teaspoon sesame oil
$1/_4$ teaspoon cayenne pepper
Freshly ground black pepper to taste
4 ounces shrimp, cleaned,
cooked, and chilled

2 large leaves Boston lettuce
1 small radish, julienned
1 teaspoon fresh cilantro, chopped
1 teaspoon fresh mint, chopped
1 teaspoon raw peanuts,
chopped

In a medium-sized bowl, combine the lemon juice, zest, oil, cayenne, and black pepper. Add the shrimp, coating well, and refrigerate for up to 4 hours.

Assembly: Place the marinated shrimp on a leaf of Boston lettuce. Add the cilantro, radish, mint, and chopped peanuts. Roll up and serve immediately.

COD WITH GRAPEFRUIT

Try to find delicious ruby red grapefruit for this dish. It will add some nice flavor to an otherwise less than exciting fish.

1 teaspoon paprika

$^1/_2$ teaspoon minced garlic

$^1/_2$ teaspoon chili powder

$^1/_2$ teaspoon dried oregano

$^1/_4$ teaspoon ground allspice

$^1/_8$ cup grapefruit juice

4 ounces cod fillet

1 cup baby spinach

1 cup baby arugula

$^1/_2$ small fennel bulb, sliced

Dressing:

$^1/_4$ grapefruit, peeled and
    sectioned

$1^1/_2$ tablespoons grapefruit juice

$^1/_2$ tablespoon sherry wine vinegar

$^3/_4$ tablespoon chopped fresh mint

$^1/_4$ tablespoon chopped fresh ginger

In a small bowl, mix the herbs, spices, and grapefruit juice. Add the cod and marinate for 30 minutes.

Place the spinach, arugula, and fennel in a medium-sized bowl. Pour all of the dressing ingredients in the bowl and mix well. Arrange on a plate and set aside.

Grill cod fillet for 3 to 4 minutes on each side until cooked through.

Serve over bed of dressed salad greens.

TUNA SALAD WITH WHOLE GRAIN MUSTARD AND WATER CHESTNUTS

Who needs mayonnaise? Certainly not you after this program. This recipe is full of flavor, but low on fat.

1 can tuna packed in spring water,
    drained

3 water chestnuts,
    coarsely chopped

1 teaspoon whole grain mustard
1 teaspoon no-fat plain yogurt

1 celery stalk, coarsely chopped
1 teaspoon freshly squeezed lemon
juice

In a small mixing bowl, combine all the ingredients.

Turkey Salad with Walnuts and Dijon Vinaigrette

*The other healthy nut. I'm not just a "one nut" kind of man. Here I add Dijon
mustard, walnuts, and green apples for the ultimate midday snack.*

4 ounces chopped fresh
    turkey breast
1 tablespoon Dijon mustard
1 teaspoon no-fat plain yogurt

$1/4$ cup chopped celery
$1/8$ cup chopped green apples
1 teaspoon chopped parsley
1 tablespoon chopped walnuts

In a medium-sized bowl, combine all the ingredients, mix well, and either
serve immediately or refrigerate.
    Serve on a bed of mesclun greens.

Low-Fat Egg Salad

*Go ahead and treat yourself! The yolk's on you! During your two-week plan,
you ate a modified version of this recipe. Here we've added an egg yolk and
some no-fat plain yogurt.*

3 hard-boiled egg whites,
    coarsely chopped
1 hard-boiled egg yolk,
    coarsely chopped
1 tablespoon no-fat plain yogurt

$1/4$ cup coarsely chopped celery
1 teaspoon wasabi powder
1 teaspoon Dijon mustard
1 tablespoon chopped fresh parsley

In a small mixing bowl, combine all the ingredients and mix well.

This is a great snack—either in the morning or the afternoon.

CITRUS TARRAGON CHICKEN

Before you say, "Not another chicken dish!" try this fresh variety. The citrus and the tarragon are a nice, flavorful addition.

$1/3$ cup orange juice

$1/3$ cup lime juice

1 tablespoon finely minced
orange peel

1 tablespoon white wine vinegar

1 tablespoon chopped fresh
tarragon

6 ounces boneless, skinless
chicken breast

Preheat oven to 350°F.

In a small bowl, combine the orange juice, lime juice, orange peel, vinegar, and tarragon. Blend well. Add chicken and coat well with marinade. Marinate for 30 minutes.

Remove chicken and place in an ovenproof baking dish. Cover with aluminum foil and bake for 30 minutes or until done.

CHICKEN AND BEAN BURGER

Beans are a healthy source of both carbs and proteins and give good substance to this burger.

$1/4$ cup canned black beans, drained

4 ounces ground chicken breast

2 tablespoons tomato sauce

$1/4$ teaspoon chili powder

$1/8$ teaspoon ground cumin

$1/8$ teaspoon salt

$1/8$ teaspoon black pepper

1 egg white, whisked

Mix all ingredients in a small bowl until well blended. Shape into a flat burger and grill until cooked through (4 minutes on each side).

Serving suggestion: Serve with Mexican Olive Salsa.

SPRING BEEF SALAD WITH BALSAMIC VINAIGRETTE

Every now and again there's nothing like the taste of lean red meat.

$1/_4$ cup diced jícama

2 teaspoons snipped chives

1 cup baby spinach

1 cup baby arugula

2 tablespoons balsamic vinegar

1 teaspoon extra-virgin olive oil

1 tablespoon whole grain mustard

Freshly ground pepper to taste

4 ounces strip steak, grilled and thinly sliced

1 spring onion, halved and grilled

$1/_2$ cup asparagus, grilled

Place the jícama, chives, spinach, and arugula in a medium-sized bowl.

In a separate bowl, combine the vinegar, mustard, and freshly ground pepper. Slowly whisk in the olive oil until well blended.

Assembly: Arrange the salad greens on a large plate. Add the onions, asparagus, and steak.

SALMON WITH GREEN APPLE

The crisp tartness of the apple complements the freshness of the salmon fillet for a tasty and satisfying treat.

4 ounces wild salmon fillet

6 green apple slices, $1/_8$ inch thick

$1/_2$ teaspoon ground coriander

Salt and pepper to taste

Preheat oven to 400°F.

Season the salmon with the herbs and arrange apple slices on top of salmon. Place the salmon on an 8-inch square of aluminum foil on a baking tray and close the packet. Bake for 8 to 10 minutes.

Serving suggestion: Serve on *Coleslaw Vinaigrette

MOROCCAN LAMB

Consider yourself transported to Morocco when you dine on this dish. The full flavor of the lamb along with the pungent flavors of coriander, cinnamon, and cumin make this a dish to savor.

1 tablespoon minced shallots

$1/8$ teaspoon cinnamon

$1/2$ teaspoon ground coriander

$1/8$ teaspoon cayenne pepper

$1/4$ teaspoon ground cumin

$1/4$ teaspoon turmeric

Salt and pepper to taste

4 ounces ground lamb

1 zucchini

Garnish: 1 teaspoon chopped
    fresh mint

Preheat oven to 350°F.

Heat a nonstick skillet over medium heat. Add the shallots, seasoning, and lamb and brown for 2 to 3 minutes.

Cut zucchini in half lengthwise and scoop out and discard seeds. Fill the zucchini halves with lamb mixture. Place on ovenproof dish and bake, covered, for 20 minutes.

Arrange zucchini halves on plate and garnish with chopped fresh mint.

7

ULTIMATE BODY
MAINTENANCE

For the past 14 days, you've pushed yourself to your limits and beyond. You've incinerated calories, sculpted sexy muscle, and burned fat. You've cleansed your body from the inside out. You've eliminated the junk from your diet and fed your body high-quality fuel every single day.

You've endured and persevered. You've overcome muscle soreness, inertia, laziness, fatigue, cravings, and addictions. You've put yourself first, prioritized your life, and stayed on track. You've lived each day in the moment, focused on what's most important to you, and kept your sights on your goal.

You may have dropped a clothing size or two or three. You're probably feeling more energetic than you have in years. Not only does your body look fantastic, but you've proven to yourself that you can do anything—literally anything—that you set your mind to. I'm proud of you, and I hope you are, too. There's no better feeling than the feeling of accomplishment.

I now must let you in on a little secret that I've been keeping from you until now. Although the past 14 days have been challenging, the true work begins today—with your body maintenance program. During the past 14 days, you may have motivated yourself by thinking, "I can do this. It's just 14 days." You may have even crossed one day after another off on your calendar. Today, however, you embark on the calendar that symbolizes the rest of your life. There are no short-term goals here. You must maintain your results permanently. As I explained before, The Ultimate New York Body Plan is a life transformation. Even if you whipped your body into top shape for a special occasion such as a wedding or high school reunion, why let your hard work go to waste after the event is over? You can continue to look fit and sexy, lean and healthy. You need only stick to the Ultimate Body Maintenance Plan.

Armed with energy, stamina, and confidence, you are ready to take on the world. Remember, I don't expect that you will strictly adhere to my A, B, C, D, E, and F of nutrition for the rest of your life. There will be times when pasta Bolognese or chocolate chip cookies win out. Don't fret; our work together will set you right back on course. Life is not a series of black-and-white vignettes where we are always surrounded by the perfect selections of food and the perfect opportunities to work out. Often, we are forced to make the best of the situation and the choices at hand. Taking this approach to the maintenance portion of my nutrition and training programs will leave you strong and empowered with the will and determination needed for a lifetime.

It will also eliminate many of the obstacles or excuses you may conjure up for not maintaining your results. You are the architect of your own destiny—embrace that concept!

The good news is that the Body Maintenance Plan is not nearly as challenging as the makeover you just completed. You won't need to work out quite so hard or quite so often. You'll be able to relax a bit on your eating—even cheat a little here and there by indulging in your favorite foods. I'd be lying, however, if I said that you could simply revert to your old ways and keep the amazing body that you just created. No, to keep that body, you must continue some of the good habits of hard work and clean eating. There's no way around it.

So promise me that you will maintain your results. Don't let this program become just another short-lived diet for you. Let it become the rest of your life. Let the rest of your life start today.

THE ULTIMATE BODY
MAINTENANCE FITNESS PLAN

To maintain your results, you must continue to exercise at least four days a week. I recommend you do the following:

- THREE DAYS A WEEK Complete your 45-minute cardio sculpting workout.

- ONE DAY A WEEK Work your pet peeves or trouble spot area—either your abs or legs and butt—with one of my toning workouts, and then follow up with 30 to 40 minutes of intense cardio.

- EVERY OTHER MONTH Switch the order of the exercise by doing the 45-minute cardio sculpting workout once per week, and work your pet peeves and other areas of your body three days per week.

Make the most of your off days. Rather than lying on the couch and watching TV, find ways to move and use your fit and strong body. Play with your kids at the park. Go for a romantic walk with your spouse. Chase the dog around the yard. Take a day hike or canoe trip. You now have the fitness and energy to explore the outdoors and suck the marrow out of life. Use all that energy you have created.

Continue to find ways to add unstructured exercise to your daily routine. Take the stairs instead of the elevator. Walk or ride a bike to your errands rather than taking the car. Walk to a coworker's office rather than sending an e-mail. All these minor movements add up over the course of the day to hundreds of burned calories.

During The Ultimate New York Body Plan, I gave you a precise description of what to do and when to do it. To maintain the best body of your life, however, you need to assume control and sit in the driver's seat. This and all my other programs center on the importance of self-empowerment. Using the tools and information that you've learned from the program, continue to explore new ways of movement. To maintain your results, you must add variety to your workouts. When you do the same workouts day in and day out, you begin to do them by rote. Your mind becomes bored, your motivation plummets, and your muscles stop responding. To keep things interesting, I suggest you periodically add new and different movements to your cardio sculpting and toning routines. As long as you stick with the basic formula of low resistance, high repetitions, you can't go wrong. If you need a bit of inspiration, check out my first book, *Sound Mind, Sound Body*, or any of my videos.

THE ULTIMATE MAINTENANCE NUTRITION PLAN

Just as you must continue to exercise to maintain your results, you also must continue to eat well. Although the Ultimate Body Maintenance Plan is not nearly so strict as the regimen you've followed for the past two weeks, you will still largely stick to your A, B, C, D, E, and F dietary rules. That said, you can safely work one or two of the A, B, C, D, E, and F items back into your diet without gaining weight. The process may take a bit of experimentation to see exactly what you can add back in—and what you can't.

Unfortunately, not all bodies are created equally, and some people can cheat more than others without seeing the results line their thighs, butt, or abdomen. Some unlucky few can barely cheat at all. To find out what you can add back in, I've broken the maintenance program into two phases, each two weeks long.

PHASE 1

In phase 1, add one daily serving of any one of the A, B, C, D, E, and Fs back into your diet. Which of the dietary no-nos you eat is up to you—and it can change every day. The main rule is that you may have only one serving. So, if you start the day with some fruit, you're done. You can't follow up with cheese, wine, or some other fattening food. Make your A, B, C, D, E, or F food choice from one of my Sound Bites lists found later in this chapter. In these lists, I've included the healthiest and least fattening options for each food category.

PHASE 2

In phase 2, add one additional serving of any the A, B, C, D, E, or F foods back into your diet, totaling two a day. During this phase, I want you to carefully monitor your weight, measurements, and clothing size and fit. Not everyone will safely be able to eat two naughty foods a day. If you start to gain weight, return to phase 1 permanently. Also, if you are extremely carb sensitive, adding certain carbs back in may set off a binge. Stay away from those foods that you've found addictive in the past. The longer you go without them, the less you'll want them.

As you add foods back in, start with the healthiest carbs first, the ones that are least likely to spike your blood sugar and send you on a binge. To do so, choose foods from my Sound Bites lists. I recommend you eat your chosen carb later rather than earlier in the day, but not past 3 P.M. Having fruit for breakfast, for example, will start your insulin levels off on the wrong foot and lead to cravings later on.

During both maintenance phases, you're allowed to have a cheat meal once a week. During this meal you can eat whatever you want. This will help keep your motivation strong for the rest of the week, reduce cravings, and prevent bingeing. If you find yourself craving a particularly naughty food, reserve it for your cheat meal. Once your cheat meal rolls around, eat guiltlessly but not mindlessly. Mindless eating—the demon that will definitely take you off track and undermine your hard work—is waiting for you at every turn. Research shows that the body will turn up the metabolism and burn off excess calories during occasional indulgences. So you can safely cheat once a week without seeing ill effects on your waistline. That said, cheating any more than one meal a week could have disastrous consequences.

SOUND BITES

The more your food resembles something that grows in nature, the better. Raw foods are better than cooked because your body must work harder to break them down. Whole foods are better than processed, for the same reason. Stick to the following Sound Bites when adding the A, B, C, D, E, and F foods back into your diet.

ALCOHOL

Alcohol is one of the trickiest foods to reintroduce to your diet. After the two-week Ultimate New York Body Plan, your body is like a clean, dry sponge. When you drink alcohol—any alcohol—your body will soak it up. You'll find that you feel bloated and your skin is puffy soon after drinking. That's why my only Sound Bite for alcohol is red wine. Red wine contains a number of nutrients that are good for your heart. It also has a rich flavor, which encourages you to drink it slowly. Finally, it contains far fewer calories and carbs than other types of alcohol.

BREAD

I have nothing good to say about bread. Even whole grain bread often contains quite a bit of white flour. Reserve bread for your cheat meal, and even then, minimize it as much as possible. For example, if ordering pizza, order a thin crust. When having a sandwich, order it open-faced with just one slice of bread. When eating out, choose just one piece of bread from the basket and then send the basket away. Sourdough bread and whole grain bread will break down somewhat more slowly than other varieties, making them slightly better choices.

STARCHY CARBS

Stick to whole grain varieties such as quinoa, lentils, beans, brown rice, and slow-cooking oatmeal. Quinoa in particular is a wonder grain that contains a high amount of protein.

DAIRY

Choose organic low- and nonfat versions of milk and yogurt. Use these mostly in recipes rather than as true meal servings. For example, use plain nonfat yogurt in place of mayo. Do not use milk or yogurt in your smoothie, as I'd rather you blend your smoothie with water. Stay away from cups of flavored yogurt, which are two banned foods in one because they contain so much sugar. The same goes for chocolate milk! Although chocolate milk is a big no-no, there are certain brands of cocoa mix that are unsweetened and taste rather delicious. Two of my favorite brands of cocoa are Ghirardelli and Dröste.

EXTRA SWEET

There's no such thing as a good sweet. Reserve sweets for your cheat day.

FRUIT AND FAT

Choose the lower carb and calorie varieties such as blueberries, strawberries, cantaloupe, kiwi, apples, and pears. Stay away from sweet tropical fruits such as papaya, mango, and pineapple. As for fats, stick to the type in oily fish such as salmon. You may also have controlled servings of nuts— about 7 to 10 as a snack. Make sure you choose healthy nuts, which are lower in fat. Raw almonds, walnuts, and organic raw peanuts are all healthy choices. The fat in flaxseed and flax oil is also very good for you.

MOVING ON

I can't believe that two weeks have passed. How do you feel? Did I deliver on my promises? You followed the workout program closely and adhered to the nutrition guidelines, and you are feeling pretty proud of yourself and your accomplishments. The things most difficult to achieve are often the most rewarding to savor. As you proceed beyond the two weeks, be mindful of the lessons you've learned and the strengths you've gained. They will serve you well in many different aspects of your life.

One of my first "makeovers," Michel, just last week told me that she recently put herself on a modified version of The New York Body Plan because she was feeling like she needed a little fine-tuning. Remember, the Plan is yours for life: It is completely transportable and easy to follow. Sam, another makeover, came into the club today and announced that he has to buy new pants because he not only has maintained his impressive results but has continued to improve on them. He said, "All my pants are falling off me."

The Ultimate New York Body Plan will provide the ultimate in mind and body transformation. Perky butts and sculpted muscles may be your initial motivation, but the ultimate prize is in the sculpting of your mind. The objective here is to gain more than just superficial beauty—which will fade in time. Because you are doing the Plan the old-fashioned way— with a lot of grit and sweat—you will be proud of the "new you" and will have greater confidence and the determination to maintain the results for life.

Self-love and self-acceptance mixed in with determination and motivation will bring about self-empowerment. These are the key ingredients to The Ultimate New York Body Plan.

Good luck, and remember that success is within your grasp.

8
RESOURCES

Throughout the pages of this book, I've mentioned many products—from stability balls to supplements—for you to buy for the best results on the program. What follows is my advice on what to look for and where to purchase each.

FITNESS EQUIPMENT

STABILITY BALLS

You'll find many brands, colors, and sizes of stability balls. Top brands include Resist-A-Ball, Duraball, Gymnic, Sissel, Gymnastik, and FitBALL. Purchase a "burst-resistant" ball in a color you like that fits your body. (See the sizing chart that follows.) You can purchase stability balls from most sporting goods stores, such as the Sports Authority and Dick's Sporting Goods. You can also find them online from the following online stores:

www.bodytrends.com
www.lifestylesport.com
www.sissel-online.com
www.resistaball.com
www.gymball.com

www.thesportsauthority.com
www.stott-pilates.co.uk
www.mensfitnessmagazine.co.uk/shop
www.fitnessaustralia.com.au/
www.activeforlife.com.au/

Medicine Balls

As with stability balls, you'll find many colors, weights, and types of medicine balls (sometimes called "heavy balls"). Choose a ball that weighs between 4 and 10 pounds, or 1 and 4 kilograms. Purchasing a ball you find both aesthetically and tactilely pleasing (a color you like and a material you like to touch) will encourage you to use the ball more often. You can purchase medicine balls from most sporting goods stores such as the Sports Authority and Dick's Sporting Goods. You can also find them online from the following stores:

www.sissel-online.com

www.bodytrends.com

www.jumpusa.com

www.lifestylesport.com

www.thesportsauthority.com

www.warehousefitness.com

www.goldsgymdirect.co.uk

www.physiosupplies.co.uk

www.mensfitnessmagazine.co.uk/shop

www.fitnessaustralia.com.au/

www.activeforlife.com.au/

Dumbbells

As with medicine balls, look for a pair of dumbbells you find both aesthetically and tactilely pleasing. Your dumbbells should weigh between two and five pounds. You can purchase dumbbells from most sporting goods stores such as the Sports Authority and Dick's Sporting Goods. Because dumbbells are durable, consider buying a used pair from eBay or another resale type of store. You can find dumbbells at the following online stores:

www.thesportsauthority.com

www.megafitness.com

www.warehousefitness.com

www.bodytrends.com

www.goldsgymdirect.co.uk

www.argos.co.uk

www.fitnessaustralia.com.au/

www.activeforlife.com.au/

Protein Shakes, Supplements, and Weight Loss Aids

Protein Powders and Shakes

Look for a protein powder or shake with no more than 5 grams net carbs and 25 grams of protein. Avoid shakes that contain artificial sweeteners, and opt for powders and shakes made from whey protein over soy, egg, and other types of protein. Also, stay away from shakes that contain maltodextrin and high-fructose corn syrup. As an added bonus, some shakes contain essential fats in the form of flaxseed oil and medium chain triglycerides, which will help to bolster energy and immunity. Purchasing a shake that contains some fiber will help to get you regular, as well.

The most important element is buying a shake or powder that tastes good. Although some powders claim you can mix them with water, I've found many of them taste palatable only if mixed with ingredients that are no-nos on the two-week program: fruit and yogurt. You can find protein powders and shakes at health-food stores, supplement stores such as GNC, and most grocery stores. If you'd like to try my personal favorite, David Kirsch's Sound Mind Sound Body Meal Replacement Powder in vanilla or chocolate, go to www.davidkirschwellness.com/oneofakindwellness You can also shop online at the following locations:

www.affordablesupplements.com
www.amazon.com/health
www.wowsupplements.com
www.shopping.com
www.theultimatenewyorkbodyplan.com

www.nutricentre.com
www.hollandandbarrett.com
www.newyorkbodyplan.co.uk
www.fitnessaustralia.com.au/
www.activeforlife.com.au/

Nutritional Supplements

On the two-week program I recommend you take supplements to make up for nutrients you may not get from your food. These include the following: calcium, vitamin B_{12}, ginseng, various antioxidants (vitamins C, E, and coenzyme Q_{10}), and fiber. You can find these supplements at most health-food and supplement stores. They are sold separately, and sometimes packaged together into one capsule. If you'd like to try the blend of vitamins and minerals that I feel work best for weight loss and increased energy and stamina—David Kirsch's Sound Mind Sound Body Vitamin Mineral Blend—go to www.davidkirschwellness.com. You can shop for nutritional supplements at the following online stores:

www.vitaminlife.com	www.nutricentre.com
www.affordablesupplements.com	www.hollandandbarrett.com
www.vitacost.com	www.newyorkbodyplan.co.uk
www.drugstore.com	www.fitnessaustralia.com.au/
www.vitaminshoppe.com	www.activeforlife.com.au/
www.theultimatenewyorkbodyplan.com	

Weight Loss Aids

I've developed a weight loss supplement combination—Flush and Cleanse, Afternoon Energy and the PM Appetite Suppressant—that contain just a hint of green tea, vitamin B_{12}, amino acids, and lots of fiber to suppress appetite and keep you regular. If you'd like to try these supplements, go to www.davidkirschwellness.com. For other supplements, you can shop online at the following locations:

www.vitaminlife.com	www.nutricentre.com
www.affordablesupplements.com	www.hollandandbarrett.com
www.vitacost.com	www.newyorkbodyplan.co.uk
www.drugstore.com	www.fitnessaustralia.com.au/
www.vitaminshoppe.com	www.activeforlife.com.au/
www.theultimatenewyorkbodyplan.com	

OPTIONAL ITEMS

Clothing

You need not purchase special clothing for the two-week plan, but you should wear clothes that feel comfortable and allow you to move with ease. If you're the type of person who tends to break a sweat, look for performance fabrics made from synthetic materials such as CoolMax and Supplex, which wick sweat away from your skin. You can find fitness clothing at sporting goods stores such as the Sports Authority and most department stores. For women, Title 9 Sports offers a wide selection of sports clothing at www.title9sports.com. Other online stores include: www.fitnessmania.co.uk, www.jjb.co.uk, www.fitnessaustralia.com.au/, and www.activeforlive.com.au/

EXERCISE MATS

An exercise mat provides a nonslip surface and a buffer between your body and the floor. You can easily roll up most types and store them behind your couch or in a closet. Look for a mat you find both comfortable and aesthetically pleasing. Make sure it is long and wide enough to cover the floor when you are lying down. You can find exercise mats at sporting goods stores such as the Sports Authority and Dick's Sporting Goods, most department stores, and the following online stores.

www.dickssportinggoods.com
www.bodytrends.com
www.matsuperstore.com
www.matsmatsmats.com
www.thera-band.com

www.goldsgymdirect.co.uk
www.stott-pilates.co.uk
www.fitnessaustralia.com.au/
www.activeforlife.com.au/

FITNESS/WELLNESS BOOKS, EXERCISE VIDEOS

- *Sound Mind, Sound Body* (Rodale Press, 2001), available at Barnes & Noble, B&N.com, Amazon.com, www.theultimatenewyorkbodyplan.com, www.nutricentre.com, www.newyorkbodyplan.co.uk and www.madison squareclub.com

VIDEOS

- David Kirsch's Ultimate Fitness Boot Camp, available on Amazon. com, www.madisonsquareclub.com, www.davidkirschwellness.com, www.theultimatenewyorkbodyplan.com, www.nutricentre.com, and www.newyorkbodyplan.co.uk

- David Kirsch's One on One Training Series, Upper Body and Abdominals, available on www.davidkirschwellness.com, www.theultimatenewyorkbodyplan.com, www.nutricentre.com, and www.newyorkbodyplan.co.uk

- David Kirsch's One on One Training Series, Legs and Butt, available on www.davidkirschwellness.com, www.theultimatenewyorkbodyplan.com, www.nutricentre.com, and www.newyorkbodyplan.co.uk

- The Ultimate New York Body Plan Video, available on www.davidkirschwellness.com, www.theultimatenewyorkbodyplan.com, www. nutricentre.com, and www.newyorkbodyplan.co.uk

INDEX